PR...
WINNING THE MENTAL GAME

"Three decades of watching the best have confirmed for me the inexorable link between success and a strong mental game. In watching Dr. Selking's work from the sidelines, *Winning the Mental Game* perfectly puts in words her artful ability to connect scientific and uniquely human practices."

MIKE TIRICO, NBC Sports Broadcaster

"*Winning the Mental Game* truly is a playbook that will help anyone translate the power of positive thinking into actionable next steps in their life."

JON GORDON, Bestselling Author of *The Energy Bus* and *Training Camp*

"Dr. Selking served as a trusted advisor to me and the Notre Dame Football program as it related to building a culture of high performance. Her expertise and wisdom, which is encapsulated in *Winning the Mental Game*, will help you and your program find layers you didn't even know you had. This foundational mental training program was taught to our players and coaches for years; it guided the mindset of our entire program, and was transformative in our approach to delivering high performance when it mattered most. This truly is *the* mental performance playbook!"

BRIAN KELLY, All-Time Winningest Head Football Coach, University of Notre Dame

"Dr. Selking has a compelling message that has been a powerful catalyst for our entire organization. She is an electric speaker who takes a complex principle like brain science and positions it so that everyone from the C-suite to our franchisees and their team members can put them into practice to become the best versions of themselves. *Winning the Mental Game* is a compilation of the core pieces of her transformative work and can help any business professional take their next step in high-performance leadership."

BETH STILLER, CEO, Massage Envy

"The better you get at your craft, the more important the mental game becomes to sustaining the excellence high-performers desire. *Winning the Mental Game* will help you elevate every aspect of your life."

BRUCE BOWEN, Three-Time NBA Champion

"There are many pretenders in the marketplace claiming to have the secrets to mastering the 'Mental Game' leading to high performance excellence, but very few actual real players; Dr. Amber Selking is the real deal, and maybe the very best of the best! Whether in sport, business, the performing arts, education, or even parenting, if you are serious about being a successful high achiever, are highly motivated and committed to producing high performance excellence, and are challenged to lead others in delivering great performance and achieving success, then you understand the critical importance of the mental game! And, you know that the mental game is a huge challenge.

You'll want to know everything that Dr. Amber Selking is sharing in her powerful new book, *Winning the Mental Game*.

She has brilliantly packaged these vital understandings, concepts, principles, strategies, and skills into a comprehensive and readily accessible program outlined in *Winning the Mental Game*. Invest in yourself—make Dr. Amber Selking's program *your* mental performance program!"

DR. RICK MCGUIRE, Retired Head Track & Field Coach and Graduate Professor, University of Missouri; Founder, Missouri Institute for Positive Coaching

WINNING
THE
MENTAL GAME

www.amplifypublishing.com

Winning the Mental Game: The Playbook for Building Championship Mindsets

@2022 Dr. Amber Selking. All Rights Reserved. No part of this publication may be reproduced, stored in a retrieval system or transmitted in any form by any means electronic, mechanical, or photocopying, recording or otherwise without the permission of the author.

Some names and identifying details have been changed to protect the privacy of individuals.

For more information, please contact:
Amplify Publishing, an imprint of Mascot Books
620 Herndon Parkway, Suite 320
Herndon, VA 20170
info@amplifypublishing.com

Library of Congress Control Number: 2021909454

CPSIA Code: PRFRE1221A

ISBN-13: 978-1-64543-618-8

Printed in Canada

This book is dedicated to that slight stirring of greatness that lies within you—may it help you fan into flame all that rests in your heart and mind.

WINNING
THE
MENTAL GAME

THE PLAYBOOK FOR
BUILDING CHAMPIONSHIP MINDSETS

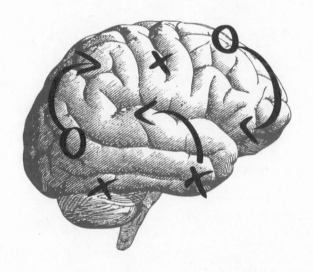

DR. AMBER SELKING

CONTENTS

FOREWORD

For me, high performance has always been about the power of a positive attitude and the discipline of personal responsibility. As a football coach, I understood the importance of training the mind and the will in our young people, and so we incorporated things like relaxation sessions, visualization, accountability, and grit long before we knew there was any real science behind it. I just knew it worked, so we did it. What this book does is put words, understanding, and training behind the very things I knew to be true as a coach, a leader, a husband, a father, and a friend. I wish I could have had this book decades ago: I could have learned and led less by trial and error, and more by intention and training!

The first time I met Amber, she wasn't a doctor yet; she was simply filled with love, passion, and determination to make a positive impact in this world. As I watched her apply herself to the development of her craft and shared a stage with her for many years at my annual Hall of Fame event in East Liverpool, Ohio, I witnessed one of the best and the brightest high-performance professionals emerge. Now, with her doctorate and loads of experiences under her belt, she remains humble and hungry, and her fire to help other people to succeed grows with every encounter we have. I signed a football for her one time with these words: "Amber, you are special. I wish I could invest in 10% of your future." Well, years later, she called me on that statement asking me to mentor her for "Year 29" of her life, as she would call it. I feel fortunate to have done so, and indeed, I view that as an investment back into our world.

This book breaks down the mental game in a way I've never seen articulated before. It goes beyond the "what" and gives you the "how" around building the strong mental performance foundation that I know leads to success. By weaving in her diverse experiences with athletes and professionals alike, this book is the real deal for anyone on a journey to become the very best they can be.

I have three rules in life:

1. Do the right thing.

2. Do everything to the best of your ability.

3. Show people you care.

Dr. Selking lives these three rules in every aspect of her life. Her wisdom is unique and powerful, and this book allows her to share that wisdom with the world. She's the best in the business at helping you and your team build the mindsets that drive positive, lasting results. So, lock in. If you can take just one thing away from this book and implement it into your life, I know you'll be a better person, leader, coach, athlete, parent, or spouse because of it.

Coach Lou Holtz
2008 College Football Hall of Fame Inductee
2020 Presidential Honor of Freedom Recipient

Thinking

BY WALTER WINTLE

If you think you are beaten, you are
If you think you dare not, you don't,
If you like to win, but you think you can't
It is almost certain you won't.

If you think you'll lose, you're lost
For out in the world we find,
Success begins with a fellow's will
It's all in the state of mind.

If you think you are outclassed, you are
You've got to think high to rise,
You've got to be sure of yourself before
You can ever win a prize.

Life's battles don't always go
To the stronger or faster man,
But sooner or later the man who wins
Is the man WHO THINKS HE CAN!

Throughout the book you'll see QR codes, which will link to additional content that supplements the text. Scan with the camera on your smart device to access podcasts, videos, and other media.

PRE-GAME SPEECH FROM THE AUTHOR

I love winning. But what I love even more is the pursuit of excellence that guides us through life in a determined and focused way. I believe we were wired for greatness—all of us. And I believe that greatness begins with how we think.

But I am frustrated, too—brokenhearted, really—when I look around and see how mediocrity and malaise pervade the lives of so many people who don't even realize that there is greatness within them. So many of us could be on the precipice of something extraordinary, but instead we choose comfort and complacency. We choose tired mindsets and broken systems over purpose, passion, and the pursuit of excellence. We stay stuck.

Yes, I said we *choose* these things. "Choice" is a powerful word; *making a choice* is a powerful action. And the beauty of choice is that we can always choose something different. **It is always within our power to choose a different way of thinking, of acting, of doing, of being**. What I've learned throughout my career, however, is that people either don't recognize *what* their choices are, or they simply do not know *how* to transform those options into *actions*.

So, this book is meant to be a bridge that will equip you to move from wherever you are right now to the next best version of who you are intended to be. This is a playbook to help you learn *the what* and *the how* of your choices in a way that allows you to tap into your greatness through a strong mental game.

When people hear what I do as a leader in the field of sport and performance psychology, their immediate reaction is often, "Oh, so you're like a motivational speaker?" I want to scream "No!" because I've found most motivational speeches and books to be lacking either in depth or in their ability to present tangible ways to translate motivational energy into not only *behavioral change*, but also *identity transformation*. The reality is, I teach science, but because I happen to have a lot of energy, it comes off as motivational! So, while I do hope this book serves as a motivational source for you, I intend even more for it to be a transformational resource that is grounded in science, helping you lay a solid foundation for a powerful approach to performance excellence. It is intended to help you win your mental game, in every aspect of your life.

*

I grew up in the small town of Montrose in northeastern Pennsylvania, where we had one stop light and more cattle than humans. Very early in life, I began to see the boxes into which people wanted to place me (and themselves), and I became committed to blasting every one of those stereotypical boxes apart. As an athlete, people wanted to label me a "jock," so I made the choice to be an athlete *and* a great student. As a Christian, people wanted to label me as a "Bible-thumper," so I made the choice to live by the Word *and* be incredibly relatable to a diverse group of people. As a country kid, they wanted to label me a "hick," so I made the choice to have small-town roots *and* city swagger.

As I matured, I realized I not only wanted to blast these boxes, but I also wanted to help bridge the gaps between the seemingly disparate "sides" that boxes create in every area of our world. Why? Because, for me, "sides" in anything are limiting and they minimize the full expression of the human experience. I believe that boxes can create constraints and stifle growth; they can make us shallow and hollow. Our differences are what make us unique and multilayered. They are important to the holistic development of excellence in people, relationships, teams, and systems.

As I reflect on my life, I see I have always been building these bridges:

- Growing up in a McDonald's franchisee family, I wanted to build a bridge between the owner/operators and the corporation because I realized the expertise and knowledge each possessed would make us even better.

- Showing livestock at the county fair, I wanted to build a bridge between the sheep barn and the pig barn because the senseless rivalries created unnecessary angst that distracted us from the amount of fun we could all have playing cards on the show boxes late into the night.

- Being a student-athlete at the University of Notre Dame, I wanted to build a bridge between the strong athletic identity we all embraced and the personal identity of the man or woman who was under that jersey because **I knew that the human could always out-perform the performer.**

- Living a life with hope in the promise of eternity, I want to build a bridge between some of the perceptions people can have of Christians as being stuffy or judgmental and the true exhilaration of a life of faith in God.

- Having friends of color whom I consider family, I want to build a bridge between different ethnicities because I know we all bleed red and that a loving, inclusive, multiethnic community is the best representation of Heaven we can create.

- Operating predominantly in male-dominated environments, I want to build a bridge between men and women because I know we are created to complement, support, and enhance one another in a variety of ways.

This pattern of being a bridge builder first became apparent to me as I left the university sport setting and entered into my first professional role. As a soccer player, I was never the most talented on the field, but I knew I would never be outworked or underestimated. It would frustrate me when I saw others who were more naturally gifted but either did not truly believe in themselves or simply chose not to work hard enough to get themselves all the way to excellence. As I moved into the corporate world, I noticed a similar dynamic. Some people seemed less gifted, but they still managed, through sheer willpower, to become great influencers, whereas others who were highly talented but lacked the drive, motivation, and discipline to be great seemed to plateau.

Recognizing such patterns in my life and the parallel performance dynamic between sport and business, I knew there must be a way to build bridges with even more intention, precision, and replicability. There must be a way to tap into human high performance, not just from a rah-rah motivational perspective, but from an empirical, evidence-based perspective, as well. There must be a science behind all of this, and it must be understood. Through my advanced degrees and subsequent applied work in sport and performance psychology, I have come to determine that the human brain is the most spectacular bridge-building mechanism there is, because from it comes our ability to think, to decide, to choose, to act, and, ultimately, to transform. And for the brain, it doesn't matter your age, race, gender, ethnicity, or socioeconomic status; it simply matters that you're human!

I began this book with the poem *Thinking* by Walter D. Wintle because, in a very real sense, my *life* began with this poem—that is to say, with the understanding that our thoughts and our mindsets are what ultimately determine how we show up for life. My mom made me memorize the entire poem when I was seven years old, and it's stuck with me ever since—not just the words, but the concepts—that our thoughts are our most powerful resource. And now, armed with the knowledge found in science and the wisdom found in Scripture, my goal in writing this book is to enhance our ability to transform our mindsets in a way that pushes us on to become the very best version of our very best selves—and all of this begins with how (and what) we think.

The values that were instilled within me as a youth, and the manner in which I have lived my life, have unfolded and manifested in a way that allows me, today, to provide people access to the boundless power and potential of their own minds. It is this boundless power, combined with a fundamental, integrated understanding of how this all works together that allows us to build championship mindsets. This book is a playbook defined as "a set of tactics frequently employed by one engaged in a competitive activity" that will teach you the eight fundamental elements of a high-performance mindset and how to employ those tactics to unleash excellence on a consistent basis.

One of the most profound experiences of my life came with the first team for whom I ever officially served as a mental performance coach. It was an inner-city boys' high school basketball team in Colorado. I was brought in mid-season because while they had loads of talent, they were disjointed, volatile, and could not seem to tap into the potential their coach knew was within them. I remember the first day I met those young men: I was dressed in business casual, my signature stiletto heels clicking on the court as I walked out to meet the team. When we first met, I could barely get them to look me in the eye. And I get it: I am a White woman who lived in a world that was completely different than theirs. But I saw it . . . I saw their greatness. And I believed in it—in *them*.

Little by little, as their coach led with poise and persistence, as they learned more about how to take control of their lives by managing their mindsets, as I met them with love and belief and confidence in who they were as young men, we formed a family—one that would "hold the rope" no matter what. And as a result, this team found new depths within their spirits *and* their game, reaching the state championship game for the first time in decades for their school. While we wound up falling just short of clinching the title, through that season we all got to wrap our arms around something that will endure far longer than any trophy ever could: one another. The tears we cried on one another's shoulders that night in that locker room will forever be etched in my heart; they still fuel the drive and passion behind my work today. Because what we also wrapped our arms around firmly throughout that season was the knowledge *and* the belief that bridges can be built in so many ways if we build them in alignment with how humans are designed to live and function optimally. We *need* each other as we journey through life. We need each other to be the best versions of ourselves so we can collectively build bridges of meaning, transformation, and excellence.

*

From a very young age, I knew I had to develop standards of excellence in everything I did in order to "be a force for good in the world," a value Notre Dame instills within its students. Now that this book has become a reality, I realize that it's been resting in me for probably most of my life. **It's been waiting to be written.**

I've devoted my life to refining, sharpening, and expanding my understanding of high performance so that it is scientifically based, empirically sound, and pragmatically applicable. People always want to talk about things like "mental toughness" and "grit" and "self-actualization."

While I believe in the importance of each of those, I have found that they are often unattainable or, at the very least, unsustainable, because so many of us lack a solid foundation upon which to really strengthen and maximize our mental game. Many of us lack a true understanding of how our brain really works, of how it influences how we show up moment by moment, and as a result, we miss the tools that position us for consistent performance excellence.

And so, **we must lay the foundation first**. This may not be the sexiest approach, but quite honestly, I'm not into sexy. I'm into excellence. And I care too much about the greatness within each of us not to give that excellence a fighting chance to thrive. So, this book will explore the **eight basic building blocks** of my foundational mental performance training program. Think of these as eight plays that make up a playbook for you to apply to every aspect of your life. These plays have been used by individuals, corporations, teams, and organizations in just about every setting from the locker room to the boardroom to the classroom to the living room.

First, to appreciate the power of the brain and mind, we will begin with some basic understanding of how they function. We will then unpack and examine the eight plays. These plays are sequential; they build upon each other. Yes, you can practice each of them separately and still achieve success, but it's when we learn to integrate them into a larger system that we unlock the key to own our performance excellence.

Each chapter will end with Championship Mindset Training, a powerful, practical exercise that will help you lay a solid mental foundation by weaving this new knowledge into the fabric of your daily life.

The goal of this book is short and sweet: to educate, equip, and empower you to become more responsible for (and to) yourself in a way that ensures you are building championship mindsets into every single aspect of your life.

As I close this section and we begin this journey toward excellence, I'm reminded of something my pastor once said: "God loves you exactly where you are, but He loves you too much to leave you there!"

I want to meet you wherever you are on your journey, whether you're taking those first, formative steps to transform your mindset or whether you're already a high achiever. Wherever you are, and whatever you're doing, *you can do it better by being better. Who we are drives what we do.* And I love ya too much to leave you on the brink of your next layer of potential! Now, more than ever, the world needs more bridge-builders, light-bearers, and hope-dealers. Now, more than ever, you need to be able to gain full access to the power of your mind and to trust yourself enough to truly believe that you can navigate the highs and lows of life to achieve your goals. Like Wintle's poem tells us, it all starts with your thoughts. Excellence begins as an inside job. You must first win in your mind.

When I'm teaching other people how to maximize their mental game, be they my elite athletes, my corporate clients, my friends, or my colleagues, this two-word call to action has become my mantra: *"Let's go!"*

So, let's go together. Let's get going on the journey to build that bridge to your next layer of greatness.

"LET'S GOOO!!!"

BRAIN SCIENCE 101

It All Begins with How We Think

---

*Do not conform to the patterns of this world, but be
transformed by the renewing of your mind.*

ROMANS 12:2

Winter had just ended in northern Indiana, so the spring sun seemed
a little extra bright and a little extra warm as I stood on the sidelines
at Notre Dame watching spring football practice. It was my first
year with the team as their mental performance coach and the first
time I had seen the student-athletes in full pads since our classroom
training sessions. The application of their newly laid mental perfor-
mance foundation had been tested in winter workouts but not yet
on a football field. As I was observing their energy, their commu-
nication, their tempo, and their ability to focus and refocus, one of
our key leaders jogged over to me. He draped his big arm around my

shoulders and said in a thoughtful tone, "Doc, I have never thought so much about what I've been thinking about. This 'mindset' stuff is blowing my mind!"

*

By the end of this chapter, I hope that you too will be thinking more intentionally about what you're thinking about. I even hope that "this mindset stuff" will "blow your mind" also. And, by the end of this book, I hope you will have laid the foundation to transform your life with the knowledge, skills, and abilities to renew your mindset in any and all circumstances.

The mind holds transformative and limitless power. What I tell all my clients, and what I'm telling you, is: **Your mind holds the key to unlocking and facilitating your transformation and moving you toward consistent, high-performance excellence. It all begins with how we think.**

I often hear people say, "Sport is 90 percent mental." While I am in the field of mental performance, and it would perhaps behoove me to advance this notion, the fact of the matter is that high-performance excellence is the combination of four domains of preparation. Whether you're competing in sports, litigating in the courtroom, balancing your company's books, raising your family, or fighting the good fight in whatever arena you may be in, these four domains are universal.

1. **Physical:** Having the physical skills and capacity to deliver the task at hand.

2. **Technical:** Having the required technical expertise, or "techniques," needed to execute your craft.

3. **Tactical:** Having the strategic understanding of whatever your "game," role, or task happens to be and knowing how to navigate it.

4. **Mental:** Having the mental skills and capacity to capitalize on your physical skillset and integrate technical skills and tactical understanding into a phenomenal performance.

While I may not overtly affirm this "90 percent mental" notion, the reality is that the mental domain does *drive* all the other domains. The term "choking" refers to the moment when an individual who *should* be able to deliver in the moment *doesn't* because all the physical, technical, and tactical training they have developed over the years gets "stuck" inside of them and cannot be released or expressed. However, when our mental domain is strong, healthy, and balanced, it optimizes the other three domains and pushes us toward high performance.

But the true power and potential of a strong mental game cannot be fully realized until we fully integrate it into *every* aspect of our lives; not only in the work we do in our professional lives but also in how we allow it to transform our minds in a more holistic sense as human beings trying to live our lives and become our very best selves. Strong mental training, then, impacts how you show up in every single aspect of your life. It is a vital part of the overall process.

Like any great building or business or family, a great mental game must be grounded in a solid foundation. And that is the intent of this book: to give you a playbook that helps you lay a solid mental performance foundation upon which you can build a consistent cognitive approach to high performance in every domain of your life. This foundation-laying process is a purposeful process; one that unfolds sequentially and with great care. Each of the eight "plays" are really building blocks that will explore a different aspect of that foundation, and each flow logically from one to the next. It is when you are able to integrate all of them that you are positioned to develop *championship* mindsets in the fullest sense. This integrative work requires discipline and open-mindedness. I have devoted my entire life to developing, honing, and spreading the importance of mental performance, which led me to designing this foundational model. I have seen how it changes lives. Now we must let it change yours.

Before we dive into the eight plays, it is critical that we have a firm understanding of at least the *basics* of brain science, as this will underscore every other element you will learn and integrate as we go. And trust me, this will be applicable in any (and every) domain of your life because what happens in the brain affects every single aspect of our existence.

The good news is this isn't rocket science; it's just brain science! While we won't be studying the intricacies of the brain in such crushing detail that you're overwhelmed, having some basic understanding will allow you to lean into the eight plays with vigor, intention, and the knowledge that mental performance training is a critical component of high-performance excellence.

Regardless of your age, race, gender, socio-economic status, life experiences, or profession, we all have a brain! So, these insights will make intuitive sense to you. They will make you say, "Wow, *that's* why this unfolded like that," or "*That's* why this thought led to that behavior." What you are about to learn will give you the courage to believe that building championship mindsets is indeed possible, even sustainable. This new knowledge will give you the sense of purpose and intention you need to move toward performance excellence in all four domains: the physical, the technical, the tactical, *and* the mental.

BRAIN GROWTH IS QUIET WORK

In just about every aspect of our lives, we can see positive results of growth clearly: you can *see* your biceps getting bigger and stronger, for example. In business, you can *see* revenues going up or costs coming down. If you're working to lose weight, a smaller waistline and pant size are the victorious whispers in your ear of "mission accomplished!"

Not so with the brain.

Unfortunately, brain growth is a quiet process, which makes it difficult to measure in an empirical sense and, therefore, difficult to discern when it actually occurs. This invisible phenomenon can be problematic when we're trying to heighten our mental performance simply because we generally don't focus on what we cannot see. It's difficult to strengthen (or even address) what is not immediately apparent. Brain growth is quiet work. And simply knowing this helps us be grittier in our pursuit of true greatness.

When brain development occurs, the signals of success are far subtler. But here's the awesome part: the results of cultivating healthy thoughts, positive mental energy, and, thus, a championship mindset are so overwhelmingly transformative they will set you on a trajectory you've never traveled before, one that perhaps you've never even realized was *possible*, much less *accessible*.

SCIENTIFIC POWER OF THOUGHT

In everything I do as a leader in the field of sport and performance psychology, and in all the principles and the practices we live by and teach at the Selking Performance Group as a high-performance consulting firm, the fundamental understanding of the power of thought stands as the solid center of our core.

When it comes to the power of our thoughts, here's what I consider to be one of the most important breakdowns: **Our thoughts affect our emotions > our emotions affect our physiological response > our physiological response is what ultimately drives our behavior and, therefore, our performance.**

I teach this powerful mental performance process and principle to all my clients because if we only get *this* right, we can change our approach to life. We need to understand and embrace the fact that our thoughts are not just ephemeral, dreamy, passive things, floating around in our heads. Our thoughts are not idle, and they are not inert. Ask any of my clients; they'll tell you how off base that characterization of thought is. They understand that **how they manage their thoughts is what drives their ultimate performance**.

Thoughts emit electromagnetic signals that wire our thinking and direct our movements and behavior. Consider this: every time you have a thought, the brain sends an electromagnetic signal; these signals are conveyed via your neurons to your muscles, and this is what directs you to execute a specific action. **The entire process begins with a thought.** And *every* thought you have matters because it's sending an electrical signal through your body to do *something*.

Thoughts → Emotions → Physiological Response → Performance

So, as we think, we must also ask ourselves, "Is this thought helping to align this mental process with success, or is it actually inhibiting it?" As high performers, we must *choose* thoughts that set this process up for success by generating the type of emotions that will in turn generate productive physiological responses that allow us to deliver our best in the moment. Because at the end of the day, only you can choose your thoughts. No one else can do that. This is your responsibility.

Consider this example. I'm walking into an incredibly important interview. I look around and see all the other candidates. Here's what unproductive thinking may look like:

- **Thoughts:** "Everyone else looks really qualified for the role. Am I good enough, prepared enough, and qualified enough to receive an offer?"

- **Emotions:** Insecurity, fear, anxiety.

- **Physiological responses:** Increased heart rate, increased muscle tension, hormonal changes (lowered testosterone, increased cortisol), visual field expands or constricts.

- **Performance:** I show up insecure, stuttering my responses, second-guessing my answers, and stiff in my body language. In other words, not optimal. (In fact, far *less* than optimal.)

If my thoughts are not in alignment with what I'm trying to accomplish—in this case, knocking the interview out of the ballpark and landing the role—then **I am not positioning myself for success**. If I'm in

 a negative mindset or if I'm allowing myself to be distracted by random, extraneous, or negative thoughts, I'm **decreasing my probability of success**, reducing my chances of accomplishing my goal. As simple as that.

THE AWESOME PART
OF BEING HUMAN

What makes us distinctly human is our unique ability to evaluate, discern, and manage our thoughts. We tend to underutilize this awesome skill and the boundless potential that lies within it even though it's ours for the taking, just waiting to be tapped. As humans, we have a brain-mind connection that is unique, unparalleled and, in my mind, *divine*.

Understanding this brain-mind connection is essential to our being able to reach the highest levels of mental performance and ensuring that these levels of excellence remain **accessible and sustainable**. Eventually, we can train our brains to seek a level of excellence that is consistently high. We can train our brains to make **excellence a habit**, a part of our daily routine.

To understand the connection between brain and mind, we must also understand the distinctions that exist between them. Sure, they're closely intertwined and this unique coupling of the two elements is what helps define us as being uniquely human . . . but as closely as they are aligned, they are also equally and distinctly different.

We are what we repeatedly do. Excellence, therefore, is not an act. It's a habit.

ARISTOTLE

BRAIN AND MIND:
UNDERSTANDING THE DIFFERENCE

The one-two punch of thoughts entering our head and then choosing what to do with those thoughts cannot be delivered unless we understand the origin of both the first punch as well as the second. One of them belongs to the brain; the other, to the mind.

The brain itself is a two- to three-pound mass of matter. The brain controls memory and speech, movement of our body parts, and the function of most organs within our body. It is a physical entity.

The *mind*, however, is the spiritual side of being human. Not spiritual in the religious sense, but spiritual in the sense that humans have a spirit or a soul, which is what makes us different than any other species, such as elephants or grasshoppers or fish or even my amazing Doberman, Rockne. Here is where we contemplate. Evaluate. Think. Process. Analyze. Think of it this way: the brain receives our thoughts . . . but the mind controls what we *do* with those thoughts. Whether we keep them, act on them, catalog them, or decide to release them is the discerning power of the mind. The mind is what allows you—as it did my athlete in the opening anecdote—to think about what you are thinking about.

There are many opinions regarding thought control. Whether we do or do not control our thoughts is not something I want to spend time debating, because here is the more important point: **our minds have the capacity to decide what to do with our thoughts once we are aware of them.**

Now that we know that we can manage our thoughts, and that thoughts can generate different emotional and physiological reactions, let's revisit our interview example. Instead of succumbing to the less-than-optimal performance brought about by all of the negative, anxiety-provoking thoughts pervading our brain, we will instead choose to release those negative thoughts and replace them with something more positive, more productive. Deliberately choosing healthy, positive thoughts will subsequently result in different emotions, different physiological responses, and therefore different performance opportunities. What unfolds this time around is something far more productive:

- **Thoughts:** "Everyone else looks really qualified for the role, but you know what? *So am I!* I have prepared for this interview, I am qualified for this job, and I am ready to join this team."

- **Emotions:** Determination, optimism, security, enhanced self-confidence.

- **Physiological Response:** Normalized heart rate, decreased muscle tension, balanced hormones, fluid visual field.

- **Performance:** I show up secure, deliberate in my responses, confident in my answers, and poised and relaxed in body language. In other words, positioned for optimization.

The reality of our scenario is that even with this enhanced mental approach, you still may not get the job. But that's not the point. The point here is that *you positioned yourself for success.* You have chosen thoughts that align your mental process toward achieving your intended outcome. There are so many variables out of your control in that moment, but if you have prepared yourself to the best of your ability physically, technically, tactically, and mentally and still come up short, you must rebound and recover quickly. You must get back to preparing for the next opportunity; back to choosing the right thoughts when that next shot comes. This playbook is intended to help you know just *how* to go about doing that.

THE POWER OF POSITIVE THINKING

I work predominantly in very male-dominated environments, and I know that many of men's initial reactions are often, "Here's a high-energy female talking about the power of positivity. Great. Let's all hold hands and sing 'Kumbaya.'" But the reality is that maximizing our mental performance and tapping into the power of positive thought involves far more than hand-holding and song-singing. Here is the bottom line about positivity and the brain: when our brain is in a positive state, we think more clearly, we think more creatively, and we problem-solve more efficiently. Our *process* improves.

Do you think this could be helpful when playing in primetime, under the lights on the football field, when you're on your own nine-yard line with less than two minutes on the clock and you need a touchdown to tie the game against the number-one team in the nation? Or in the court room when delivering a closing argument in a critical case? Or at the end of the month when trying to hit those sales targets? Or even at home when navigating family challenges? Like it or not, our brains are designed to function most optimally when they are in a positive state. Positive thinking is not something soft and fluffy. Positive thinking is a science-based, performance-enhancing strategy.

It is for this reason that I challenge leaders, executives, coaches, teachers, parents (i.e., anyone who is trying to create a positive and productive experience) to start meetings on a positive note. At the beginning of each meeting, ask people to share recent wins, to report whatever creative ideas or innovative thoughts they've been considering, or to simply recount aloud the best part of their week. Yes, this positive sharing helps build relationships, but it also primes everyone *mentally* to get down to business and tackle the challenges and opportunities before them.

I know there are some of you who are probably still balking at this idea of positive thinking as a scientific concept. So, let's just remove the word "positive" for the time being. Instead of positive thinking, let's call it *productive* thinking, or *right* thinking. These are all synonyms for positive thinking, of course, but they are also helpful because they are antonyms for negative, unproductive, or wrong thinking. Don't allow yourself to miss this subtlety on the grounds of semantics: the power of positive thinking is not an empty aphorism. Don't allow yourself to be so easily distracted from the path of high performance. These concepts are critical. Try to open yourself to them fully. So, this definitely bears repeating: **we can choose what we do with our thoughts, and productive thoughts will impact our ultimate performance**.

THE BRAIN AS A MUSCLE

Thoughts are important because they send electrical signals through our bodies. They are also important because they are the starting point of the mental performance process. But thoughts are even *more* important because through repetition they build mindsets, and **mindsets determine how we show up for life, moment by moment.**

While the brain is not a muscle in the scientific sense, it functions like a muscle in that the *parts of it that we use*, the parts of it that we exercise and train, grow and become stronger. The parts of it we do not use get weaker. Look at it like this: **thoughts are mental reps for your brain.** Just as our biceps can get bigger and stronger through repetitions with weights, mindsets also grow bigger and get stronger through repetitions of thought.

A mindset, then, is simply a patterned way of thinking; thoughts that we have repeated so often that they are woven into our very brain matter. Mindsets are actual protein patterns that alter the form and function of our brain and determine how we see ourselves, how we move through the world, and how we stand up, suit up, and show up for life.

We might not always realize it, but we have mindsets about everything. Stop for a moment and reflect on some of your own mindsets:

- How do you think about what town, city, or country you are from? What does this mean to you and what does it say about you from your perspective? These repeated thoughts reflect your current mindset about where you are from.

- How do you think about your age, gender, race, or religion? What do these things mean to you? These repeated thoughts represent your current mindsets about some of the core elements of your demographic identity.

- How do you think about the groups with whom you are affiliated? Your team, or your company, or your family, for example? These are your current mindsets about the groups with whom you interact.

By now, you are becoming more aware of your thought process (i.e., thinking about what you're thinking) and your ability to control and direct your thoughts. You may even be evaluating your current state of success and steadfastness, attributing them to the mindsets you've built over your life. Or, you may feel a little disheartened or even disturbed when you consider the unhealthy mindsets you've been subconsciously wiring into your brain over the years.

While it would be ideal if we all have positive, optimistic, confident, peaceful, loving mindsets toward ourselves and others, the reality is that many of us also have negative, pessimistic, insecure, anxious, and even disdainful mindsets toward ourselves, others, and the world around us. Negative mindsets do, indeed, exist.

Take heart! The beautiful part about the human brain is that what we wire in, we can also wire out. Just as our muscles will atrophy when we stop working out, our mindsets and thought patterns can atrophy, too, in a sense. This means it is within our control to dissipate and diffuse negative thought patterns (mindsets) when we stop repeating the thoughts that have constructed them. This is the concept of **neuro-plasticity** in a nutshell: new neural connections and pathways can be formed or reformed based on what we think about!

People with positive mindsets are generally people who think clearly. Creatively. Boldly. Who problem-solve and self-correct. Who stand in the center of their own self-confidence, and if they stray from that center (and let's face it, we *all* stray at some point or another), they're equipped with the tools, the techniques, and the knowledge to steer themselves back on track.

But just as we must intentionally and consistently train our body if we want it to be fit and physically conditioned, we must also train our mind through our thoughts if we want to keep in optimal mental and emotional condition. And here, another critical point: **high-performance thinking can be learned, and high-performance mindsets can be built**.

Through our work together, my clients *learn* how to think positively (aka, productively), even amidst adversity, failure, and challenge. They *learn* how to cultivate a positive mindset that is sustainable rather than fleeting. They *learn* how to repeat these mental patterns, whether they're on the field or off. They *learn* that their mindset is what will ultimately lead them to high performance, not just in their sport or business, but in the much more expansive and important game of *life*. This is what building championship mindsets is all about!

That we are, as I write this book, in the clutches of a global pandemic and in the midst of racial and social unrest, even those of us who are the most positive thinkers recognize that there is plenty in the world to be negative about. But now, perhaps more than ever, is the time for positive thinking and forward-moving momentum, not just as individuals, teams, and corporations, but as a nation and a world bound together, collectively. Positivity does not always mean happy; it means optimistic, with the belief that there is indeed a plan, a future, and a shot at redemption.

How do we maximize the benefits of a productive mindset? I've developed a three-step process that has proven extremely successful in helping my clients establish one. I share it here, right at the very beginning of the book, so you can start using it immediately as we begin our journey and as we all seek the redemptive power of a renewed mind.

Recognize → Replace → Radiate

Step 1: Recognize. We must recognize when our mindsets are or are becoming unproductive. We must become aware of the thoughts we are thinking so we can make the choice to intentionally move forward toward unity and high performance.

Step 2: Replace. Our capacity to replace negative or unproductive thoughts with positive, productive thoughts is what makes us uniquely human. We have within us the ultimate power (and capacity) to replace negative energy with positive, despair with hope, emotional chaos with calm, and hate with love. And, like our muscles, if we choose to exercise them, these thought patterns will only grow stronger with use.

Step 3: Radiate. Both the heart and the brain emit electromagnetic signals and energy. It has been reported that heart energy can actually radiate from a person as far as ten feet outward. You've heard of a person emitting "positive" and "negative" vibes? Well, it is our mindset that drives our "heartset." What we choose to think about will generate heart energy that impacts those around us. My hope is that rather than wickedness and mediocrity, we will all make the *personal choice* to radiate goodness and greatness.

Remember, **we choose our mindsets; we should not let our mindsets choose us**. With the basics of brain science set as a solid base, we can now begin laying the foundation that will allow you to construct your own championship mindsets. The eight plays of this playbook, the building blocks that comprise that substructure are:

1. Awareness – You must be aware before you enhance.

2. Motivation – It is your job to motivate yourself.

3. Confidence – It's a choice.

4. Intensity Management – Find your optimal zone.

5. Attentional Control – You give power to what you focus on.

6. Emotional Mastery – Control the controllables.

7. Mental Rehearsal – What the mind conceives, the body achieves.

8. Routines – How you do anything is how you do everything.

These eight mental performance plays, these vital building blocks, taken together in a holistic and fully integrated sense, will ensure you are better educated, better equipped, and more empowered to take responsibility for your own life, your own situation, and, ultimately, your own success, at whatever level you choose.

So, without further ado . . . LET'S GOOO!!

CHAPTER ONE

PLAY #1:
AWARENESS

You Must Be Aware Before You Enhance

---

*I think self-awareness is probably the most
important thing towards being a champion.*

BILLIE JEAN KING

Exhausted, he sat before me with hopeful eyes. My client had come for help figuring out why he felt so tired all the time. As an up-and-coming young corporate executive, he was used to being vibrant, full of life, and mentally sharp. But with his new role, he found himself in the public spotlight far more often, leading meetings instead of just being a participant, and having people recognize him at dinners and social events.

After some basic personality profiling, which we do with all our clients, I asked him, "How much alone time do you get?" He looked at me inquisitively and said, "Not much. I don't really need it." It was clear from his assessments that he was an introvert, and at certain thresholds needed to be alone to recoup his energy. He assured me that he enjoyed being around people and that he wasn't afraid of speaking or engaging others; because of these things, he had always believed he was an extrovert. But when he became aware of the fact that introversion and extroversion have less to do with your comfort level around people and more to do with how you generate your energy (the former from quiet, reflective time alone and the latter from being around others), it clicked in his head why he felt drained and distracted. It began to make sense. In his previous role, that restorative time was naturally built into his day; in his new role, there was rarely a time when he found himself alone.

As he began creating more personal space and time to reset, refocus, and reenergize (not a lot, but just enough), his energy returned, his sense of control increased, and he began believing again that he was in the right place, doing the right work, around the right people. He became more aware of his own personal wiring, and as a result, he was able to enhance who he was and how he showed up to the people and responsibilities around him.

*

Awareness itself sits at the center of all of this. If we are not aware of how we are wired, if we are not aware of our thoughts and behaviors, and if we don't recognize our power to manage and redirect our thoughts so that they remain positive and productive, we are limiting our ability to perform excellently. It all begins with awareness.

This is why awareness is a vital part of each of the next seven plays we are about to examine and why it is positioned as the very first of the eight. We can't really run the other seven plays until we learn this one. To grow stronger, to get better, to show up for life, and to adapt to changing and challenging circumstances, *awareness must rule*. By that I mean we must become vitally aware of every aspect of our living, and we can't really begin this journey toward excellence and high performance until we are fully aware of where we stand at this very moment. Remember that **you must be aware before you can enhance**. It all begins with awareness.

Think back to a scene I described in the previous section. Let's go back to that sparkling afternoon at spring practice on the Notre Dame football field, when one of our key players jogged off the field and spoke to me about his newfound level of awareness. Remember his words? "Doc, I have never thought so much about what I've been thinking about. This 'mindset' stuff is blowing my mind!" What was "mind-blowing" was the power of his own personal awareness and how invigorating it felt to have this awareness manifest in his life, both on the field and off. What it boils down to is this: he was becoming more aware of his awareness, and it was beginning to feel empowering and transformative. This is what awareness will do.

Understanding that awareness underpins the very foundation of high performance, we position ourselves to more deeply and intimately understand and explore each of the next seven building blocks. As we move sequentially through each of them, we will equip ourselves with the tools we need to direct and redirect our thoughts, manage our minds, and push toward the next level of performance excellence that is attainable and, yes, sustainable.

THE FUNDAMENTALS
OF AWARENESS

High performers of any kind, in any industry, profession, or business, are always incredibly aware of all aspects of their body, their mind, their heart, and their environment. This heightened awareness makes them sensitive to the ways in which they need to adapt, improve, and recover, and it enables them to continue to perform at consistently high levels in any and all situations.

Eventually, we can bring these adaptive capabilities to every moment of our lives in a way that is meaningful and lasting. This is what will allow us to suit up and show up for life with purpose, precision, and a clear-sighted understanding that we can, and we must, control and direct this process. Yes, awareness belongs to each of us . . . but we must reach out and grab it for ourselves. Only then can we integrate these practices and principles into our own lives in a way that makes sense and makes a positive difference. No one else can do it for us.

The beauty of awareness is that it can meet you wherever you are. If you're already a high performer and you want to push your performance to even greater heights, or you're relatively new to the game and eager to explore and tap into these principles, it all begins here. No matter your background, your profession, or your area of interest, our awareness is what makes us uniquely human. Awareness is the great equalizer.

You've heard me say this before, but it bears repeating, especially at the outset of this important chapter: before you can get better at anything, **before you can change or improve any aspect of your life, you must be aware of your current situation**, and your assessment of your situation must be brutally honest. It must be raw and uncompromising. It must be rooted in truth, grounded in fact. This assessment will help sharpen your vision, not just of where you are now, but where you eventually want to be, and what you need to do to get there. *This kind of vision is vital.* Why? Because without vision, people perish. Without vision, we have no sustainable sense of direction, physically, technically, tactically, or mentally. You must be aware of every aspect of your life before you can enhance any aspect. Let's first understand the scientific underpinnings of awareness. This shouldn't come as a surprise: **it begins with the brain**.

THE SCIENCE OF AWARENESS

When we repeat certain motions, patterns, or thoughts, they will eventually become "automatic." When athletes, for example, execute a single motion repeatedly, they are eventually able to execute that motion without giving it much thought. This is when the cognitive processing for the execution of that action moves from their conscious brain to their subconscious brain. When an act, a task, or a thought requires less conscious effort and mental processing to execute, it is known as **automaticity**.

Let's use a more practical example. Remember when you first learned to drive a car? You devoted all your energy and attention to the task of driving. You were zeroed in, right? You carefully positioned both hands on the steering wheel at 10:00 and 2:00. You probably checked your mirrors constantly, gave careful thought to putting the car into gear, and always eased into traffic with great care. But the more you drove, the better you became, and the less conscious thought was required to perform the task. You had reached a level of automaticity. When this happens, more "room" is created in the conscious brain to process other information and think about other things. This is known as **parallel**

processing. Now your conscious brain has the additional capacity to process more nuanced situations and scenarios; more room to absorb, analyze, and utilize additional data in a way that enhances your performance and expands your levels of awareness and adaptability. Now you could begin to redirect your conscious thoughts elsewhere. For example, while you drive your car, you can have a conversation with the passenger or sing along with a tune on the radio, or think through the major points of the presentation you're about to give, or even remind yourself to pick up that loaf of bread on your way home later in the day. Because you've gotten good at it, less mental processing and deliberate thought is required to actually drive the car, and you have conscious space to process other things.

Automaticity and parallel processing give the conscious brain additional room to take in, analyze, and use much more data internally and externally to achieve the performance excellence you desire. Understanding these scientific principles sets us on a firm foundation and shows us that, through training and mental discipline, we can increase our awareness of and, therefore, attention in the present moment in a way that enhances our overall performance at every level.

This is vital information and critical knowledge, especially when you consider that we have as many as 70,000–80,000 thoughts per day. Being aware of what we're *doing* with those thousands of thoughts in terms of directing, controlling, managing, and maximizing them so that they become a *positive* force is vitally important.

What is necessary to change a person is to change his
awareness of himself.

ABRAHAM MASLOW

THE FIVE ASPECTS OF AWARENESS

There are five different aspects of awareness that, when understood and utilized, will prepare us to capitalize on the next seven building blocks most effectively. It's important to remember that deliberate training in these areas and developing a willingness and ability to apply these principles in your own life in a purposeful, disciplined manner can enhance your journey toward performance excellence.

1. PHYSICAL AWARENESS

High-level performers in *any* domain know their bodies extremely well. Having this intimate familiarity with our bodies—our physical strengths and weaknesses, the feel of various movements, the sensation of our bodies as they move through space—allows us to adapt, improve, and recover from difficult or challenging situations. Being physically aware also means being aware of your energy levels. Knowing when you need to hydrate, eat, or rest plays into your ability to perform at the very top of your game *at all times.*

We must know our physical selves. I'll use myself as an example. After sustaining a knee injury that ultimately ended my soccer career at the University of Notre Dame, I decided to try boxing. When I was in the ring, my fight name was "BulletProof Tiger." And when I suited up for a fight, put my gloves on, got my mind right, and stepped into that ring to face my opponent, I really did *feel* like a bulletproof tiger. I felt fierce. Fast. Strong. Focused. But I was also aware of something else: I tended to carry stress and tension in my traps (trapezius muscles are in your shoulder/neck). This simple awareness that I carried tension in certain parts of my body ultimately improved my performance in the ring by helping me adapt, adjust, and perform at maximum capacity.

I was aware that holding tension in my traps was preventing me from throwing a full, strong, clean punch, and this awareness is what led me to change my behavior. Being aware of this fact allowed me to adapt and improve; it reminded me to keep my traps relaxed, which in turn allowed me to get into a stance to execute and position myself to be successful. And this vital awareness ultimately made me a better boxer.

When we become more physically aware of what our bodies are doing (or not doing), it allows us to make the necessary adjustments. All of this is completely within our control; we just have to be aware enough, and present enough, to push ourselves toward this level of adaptability.

Heightened physical awareness also allows us to slow our movements so that we can *learn* from them. This happens with elite athletes all the time. When an athlete slows down his or her movements, it allows them to learn new skills accurately and make adjustments more efficiently. It allows us to manage our bodies accordingly and use our mental skills to stay in the game. Slowing our movements (and sometimes our thoughts) enables us to absorb and integrate new information more purposefully. If we try to do everything at full speed right away, we often miss the nuanced details. One of the collegiate football coaches with whom I work often tells his guys, "This is learning speed, not game speed," when he introduces a new drill. Once they get the hang of it and demonstrate proper technique, *then* they increase the speed of the drill.

Having an awareness of tension, pain, or imbalance in any part of your body allows you not just to address the imbalance directly and specifically, but to release that imbalance so that you can perform more freely, just as I did when I was in the boxing ring.

Establishing and maintaining a heightened physical awareness is important in any domain and in every profession. When you become more aware of your physical energy and your physiological reactions, particularly in high-stress situations, it allows you to proactively manage negative and/or unproductive thinking and behavior.

When I work with clients, I help them become more aware of their patterns of behavior. I help them recognize when their energy levels are highest, for example. When do they tend to think more clearly? What time during the day does their attention level tend to nosedive? Being aware of these physical dynamics allows them to schedule their day around the moments and spaces of time when they are most productive. This awareness, then, helps us identify (and even create) our periods of peak performance, which ultimately drive us to higher levels of excellence and productivity.

2. MENTAL AWARENESS

High performers in any domain are also keenly aware of their thoughts, their thought patterns, and their mindsets. This is essential—not just because we have 70,000–80,000 thoughts throughout the day—but because mental awareness allows us to identify the thoughts that help our performance and identify the thoughts that hurt our performance. It also allows us to manage those thoughts in a way that facilitates our performance. Consider the following as a perfect example of what happens when we enhance our mental awareness.

Once, I was doing a Mental Performance Training (MPT) session with a baseball team. As part of the training, I asked the players to write down on notecards whatever negative or unproductive thoughts they might be having when they step into the batter's box. I then asked them to pass their cards to the teammate sitting next to them so their teammate could help change that negative thought into a more positive, productive thought. (Because we all know that it's usually easier to help *other people* think positively than it is to push ourselves in that direction, right?) When they were finished, I asked for volunteers to share. One young man raised his hand enthusiastically and said, "Excuse my language, Doc, but what I'm really thinking when I walk up to the plate is, 'Oh, shit! I hope I don't strike out.'"

It's easy enough to understand that this young man was probably feeling more than a little nervous and stressed as he walked to the plate. He's anxious. His heart rate is up. His field of vision is constricted, his testosterone (the power hormone) has probably plummeted, and his cortisol levels (the stress hormone) have probably started to spike. So, he is not in a good place. He has not optimally positioned himself to get a hit. When I asked him how his teammate had recommended changing the trajectory of his unproductive thinking, he smiled, issued yet another apology for the language, and answered with bright enthusiasm, "Well, now, instead of 'Oh, shit,' I'm gonna be thinking, 'Okay, I *got* this shit!'"

So now, because of this heightened mental awareness of the thoughts he had as he approached the plate and his ability to adjust his negative thinking, he's probably going to walk up to the plate with just a little more swagger, a double dose of confidence, authority, and can-do spirit. And what's more, not only will his performance improve but the overall performance of the entire team will improve as well.

This is a powerful example of how quickly we can change our thoughts, how efficiently we can redirect our thinking so that we can influence the overall trajectory of our behavior and, therefore, performance.

Most people wage a constant battle between managing their negative and their positive thoughts. (Remember that "negative," "unproductive," and "wrong" are all synonyms, as are "positive," "productive," and "right.") Unfortunately, most people allow negative thoughts to dominate their thinking. This is problematic and destructive, of course, because if we've got negative thoughts running through our mind, they affect our emotions, which in turn affect our body's physiological response. So, we've got to be aware of our thoughts so that we can make sure we have ones that facilitate our performance rather than hinder it. This is when we can more fully position ourselves for success. And who controls what you do with your thoughts? You do! No one else. This job belongs to you and you alone, but it's my job throughout this book to help get you there!

3. EMOTIONAL AWARENESS

First, let's understand that no single emotion is necessarily bad in itself. Each emotion is relevant and perhaps even necessary. Anger and anxiety, for instance, while uncomfortable, are simply important indicators of something larger at play. It is our *response* to these emotions that can have a negative or positive impact on our ultimate performance. So, it's not the emotion that matters necessarily, but our response to it. The good news is that how we respond to our emotions is completely within our control. Consider this example:

I worked with an executive who, in negotiations, tended to bring his negative emotions to the table. When this happened, he could feel his body temperature rise and his heart rate increase; of course, this all had a negative effect on his overall performance as a negotiator. Once we started working on his awareness, once we started the mental training and practice, he began to realize that he could actually manage those emotions and even redirect them when they surfaced by managing his thoughts. Remember: our thoughts affect our emotions, which affect our physiology, which ultimately drives our performance. By pausing to consider the *thoughts* that were triggering his emotional responses, he was able to adjust his thinking to adjust his emotional reactions.

Now when he sat down at the table, he was able to be calm, composed, and in control because his thoughts were facilitating those emotions. He no longer let his emotions rule his behavior. As a result, he became a more effective, strategic negotiator. It was his awareness, then, that allowed him to adapt. And along with this enhanced awareness came the shining recognition that he no longer needed to be held captive by his emotions. Instead, he could become the master of them! This is how emotional awareness drives us toward performance excellence.

This is crucial information, particularly because most of us are more aware of and sensitive to our emotions than we are most other things in our life. We are attuned to our emotions because they are a manifestation of our thought life. We know when we're angry, for example, because we *feel* it. Our pulse quickens. Our body temperature rises. Our thinking becomes more intense. Emotions are visceral and deeply personal—especially negatives ones—and if we are angry or anxious, for example, you better believe we are fully aware of that anger or anxiety.

But if we're not careful, we can let our emotions take control and direct our behavior in negative, unproductive ways. Again, we must remember that we alone hold the reins. Your life is too important to be swayed by the whims of emotional feelings; how you show up to the

moment is too critical to be derailed by the flash in your gut and flutter in your heart. We must allow our emotions to be indicators of the situation at hand, and then choose thoughts that can massage those emotions into the most productive response.

4. SITUATIONAL AWARENESS

High performers in any domain or profession are able to absorb tremendous amounts of information from their surroundings. Having a heightened situational awareness allows us to evaluate our options more quickly and more efficiently; it enables us to make better decisions—often in the heat of the moment—and it increases our reaction time. All of this, of course, is based upon strong scientific underpinnings. Let's look at an example of someone who displays consistently excellent situational awareness.

Peyton Manning is a two-time Super Bowl Champion and former NFL quarterback for the Indianapolis Colts and Denver Broncos. His situational awareness skills are *extraordinary*. When Manning stood at the line of scrimmage and the ball was about to be snapped, his ability to take in the entire situation around him was incredible. He saw *everything*, down to the finest detail that any average NFL quarterback may miss. Because he saw everything, including the slightest shifts in the defensive coverage that he picked up as he scanned the defense, he called an audible, changing the play at the very last second and leaving the defense to scramble to adjust. This is why he is legendary: he saw what other people could not see. By doing so, he was able to maximize his own performance and, equally important, the ultimate performance of his entire team. His unusually high level of situational awareness (derived from his insatiable tactical preparation) allowed him to execute at an extremely high level from anywhere on the field. This is what situational awareness is all about. Manning had been studying and executing this game for a long time; in this sense, he reached an extraordinary level of both automaticity and parallel processing, which freed his conscious brain to absorb and process tiny details and small nuances that others may have missed. This is situational awareness at its very best.

5. DYNAMICS AWARENESS

This is a fairly expansive category. This could refer to relational dynamics (personal or professional relationships), power dynamics, industry dynamics, and so on. Basically, this is being aware of the systems of which you are a part that allow you to optimize your role and presence within a broader structure. This is the level of awareness that allows you to recover better (and faster) after encountering a challenging or disheartening experience because when you know the broader game "at play," it makes more sense why certain things may happen and we tend to not take them so personally.

When we understand the power dynamics that are in play within different systems, group structures, or organizations, we can navigate them more wisely, more adeptly, and more strategically. We grant ourselves more time to think through how we're going to operate, how we're going to show up at any given moment, and how we ourselves will function most efficiently within this larger group dynamic.

Consider this example. Mergers and acquisitions of companies provide a plethora of dynamics to analyze, understand, and capitalize upon. Whether they are the dynamics of the companies' historical and cultural journeys to date, any power struggles between the leadership teams of the target company and acquiring company, or industry factors that operate on different cycles, a *lack* of awareness of these dynamics can undermine the entire integration process. According to the *Harvard Business Review*, 70 to 90 percent of all mergers and acquisitions fail, and I propose that many of these failures occur from lack of dynamics awareness before, during, and after the acquisition.

But also remember this: **even within a larger group dynamic, you are the one who controls your thoughts.** You and only you. This is an important nuance. You can still be the calm in the midst of chaos.

Awareness is like the sun: When it shines on things,
they are transformed.

ECKHART TOLLE

FROM AWARENESS
TO MOTIVATION

It's worth repeating this principle again, and I will continue reiterating it throughout the book: *we have to be aware before we can enhance.* This is why awareness itself is the underpinning of every building block in our foundation, of every "play" in our playbook.

As we begin to raise our awareness levels—physical, mental, emotional, situational, and dynamics awareness—something else begins to happen: we create a cognizance that allows us to ask ourselves such questions as, "Are the things that drive me from day to day, from moment to moment, big enough, provocative, and substantial enough to get me through difficult or challenging moments?" This is where motivation, our second mental performance play, comes in.

You're probably now beginning to understand why these plays are sequential, how they build upon one another and are, each of them, based on a solid, scientific foundation. But before we move to motivation, let's end this chapter on awareness with a Championship Mindset Training (CMT) exercise. Try it out in your own life and begin to practice these principles daily.

PLAY #1:
AWARENESS

CHAMPIONSHIP MINDSET TRAINING:
"Well, Better, Learned"

———

At the end of every day, get into the habit of asking yourself a short, simple list of reflective questions. Write down your answers so that you can reflect on them later; writing them down will allow you to chronicle your own growth. You can even jot down the answers in this book—I want you to use this as a workbook and a practical roadmap; indeed, a playbook. Answering these questions will help set you on the path to enhanced awareness, which will set you on the path toward performance excellence. Ready? Let's go!

1. What **three things** went well today, and *why* did they go well?

2. What **two things** need to get better tomorrow, and *how* will I make them go better?

3. What is **one new thing** I've learned about myself today, and *why* is that important?

CHAPTER TWO

PLAY #2:
MOTIVATION

It Is Your Job to Motivate You

---

*The will to win, the desire to succeed, the urge to reach
your full potential . . . these are the keys that will
unlock the door to personal excellence.*

CONFUCIUS

When I got my first college football consulting opportunity, I was still in graduate school. A head coach called me to walk his Division-I staff through a half-day high-performance session. I prepped for weeks. I knew walking into that meeting there would be more than 240 years of combined coaching experience sitting around the table.

I knew being young *and* female would present two potential barriers to winning their buy-in, but I trusted my gut and opened with one of the most critical questions we can ever ask ourselves as humans: *Why?*

"Why do you coach?" I asked them and told them to write down their answers. The resistance I had seen when I began the session, evident in their facial expressions and body language, slowly started to transform into genuine interest as they began to reflect on . . . to remember . . . *why* they still coached football after all these years. As they began to share their reflections and the discussion around the table among these men became more animated, you could see and feel the hard shells of masculinity begin to soften and the flicker of full engagement begin to re-ignite. From there, our time together passed incredibly quickly, and they requested we extended our session by another two hours. By the time the day concluded, we knew the head coach's purpose for the day—aligning coaches from the offensive and defensive sides of the ball—had been fulfilled by their remarks of mutual respect and anticipation for the future during our debrief session.

*

From this example, we begin to feel the interrelated connection between awareness and motivation, and we develop a stronger foundational understanding of a concept that's hopefully beginning to feel familiar: **we must be aware before we can enhance.**

It all begins with awareness. As we move to this second play of motivation, consider this connection, too: before we can motivate ourselves to *be* better, to *stay* better, and to push past (and learn from) our weaknesses and vulnerabilities, we must be aware of how our thoughts affect our emotions and how our emotions influence our behavior. When your awareness levels increase, you can better direct and redirect your thoughts so they remain positive and productive, even (perhaps *especially*) during times of challenge and adversity. This is where motivation comes into play.

When you are motivated, driven, and constantly propelled toward being (and becoming) the next best version of yourself and you understand precisely where the passion to excel is coming from, then you commit to doing the things necessary to learn, grow, and get better at your craft. People share their dreams and goals with me all the time, but, honestly, I am always more interested in learning how badly they want to accomplish them. I care about what they want, but I care even more about what they're willing to *do* to get what they *say* they want. Motivation is the fuel to get there.

IT'S YOUR JOB TO MOTIVATE YOU!

Awareness and motivation are also closely tied because they share some of the same properties. Like awareness, motivation—if it is to be sustainable, anyway—must come from within. **It is your job to motivate you.** It must begin as an inside job. Just as it is your job to choose and manage your thoughts, it is your job to continually find ways to propel yourself onward. Yes, there are external forces that can serve as effective motivators (think of the coach who demands precision during practice drills, or the parent who ensures his child studies for that upcoming test), but these external motivators, as helpful as they might be in the moment, are not sustainable. The drills and exams will eventually end, and these young people will be expected to go to work consistently, contribute in their communities, and build healthy relationships. If they have only learned to "deliver" when prodded by their parent, teacher, or coach, a sense of entitlement or delusion about the reality of how the world works can pervade. There will *always* be the next challenge, the next game, the next hurdle, the next test; this is why motivation that comes from deep within is what will ultimately optimize your performance in a way that *endures*, regardless of external factors. Motivation that is internally driven is what will keep you propelled, buoyant, and on course as you navigate the waters of life, across any domain and every spectrum.

BEGIN WITH THREE CRITICAL QUESTIONS

1. *Why* am I doing what I'm doing?

2. What do I want to *accomplish* from doing this?

3. How do I want to be *remembered* when I am gone from this experience or season of life?

Understanding the answers to these three key questions will keep you purpose-driven, clear-sighted, and continually motivated—even during moments of challenge, anxiety, and adversity. It is during such times when the ability to dig deep and draw strength from within is most important and can create the greatest opportunities for growth. These are the questions to which we must continually return because they will keep us on a motivational path, even (perhaps especially) when our balance might be a little off, our energy level might be a little low, and our anxiety level might be a little high. We must remain focused on what matters to us the most, versus simply how we may feel in the moment. These questions serve as a kind of North Star in our lives, and it is not just the act of asking ourselves these questions but the act of thoughtfully listening to our answers that will keep us grounded, focused, and moving forward.

Throughout the course of any day, I ask myself these questions simply because the very act of "checking in" ensures that I remain in full alignment with (and constantly aware of) my mission and, ultimately, my "why." Being able to articulate and identify a clear reason and purpose for your actions, i.e., knowing what stands at the center of your "why," is what helps drive performance excellence, even on the days when you may not *feel* like striving for excellence. It is on those low-energy, off-balance days, when "just okay" seems preferable that learning to draw on motivation becomes the most critical.

Many people without the correct mental training, or those who have not yet developed a championship mindset, believe that if they can't give 100 percent, they are done playing. They are out of the game. If they can't give it everything, they'd rather not give anything. They give some comfortable excuse, walk away, and tell themselves they'll come back when they're more confident and more fully equipped to hit their 100 percent mark. They cut corners and justify their lack of effort. But here's the point: high performers simply give 100 percent of whatever they have to give. Excellence is about incremental growth and commitment over time, not perfection.

For those of us who tend to have this all-or-nothing mindset, wrapping our heads around this concept can be a bit tricky. As a soccer player at Notre Dame, my workouts were a minimum of an hour and a half of intense training. When I retired from playing after multiple knee surgeries, there were very few days when I could spend that amount of time working out because I filled the void soccer had left with other important priorities. I deluded myself that shorter or less intense workouts were of little to no value at all and didn't constitute a full workout, so why bother?

Eventually, though, I *learned*. Eventually, I adjusted this mindset. It took purposeful effort. It didn't happen accidentally; it unfolded as a result of a heightened awareness. As I developed this new mindset and cultivated these new thought patterns, my overall approach to performance excellence expanded. Here's what I came to believe: if 70 percent was all the capacity I had in me at that time, then, darn it, I was going to give 100 percent of the 70 percent I had! Why? Because, at the end of the day, 70 percent is greater than 0 percent, which is what I would have given had I allowed my limitation to determine the outcome.

It is all about giving 100 percent of whatever you happen to have within you, even if that's only 70 percent, or 30 percent, or 10 percent. That requires motivation. As long as I gave all of what I had to give, even if it was 50 percent less than my past potential, I was doing everything I possibly could to succeed. Eventually, I learned to see this not as a failure (we'll examine failure in more detail in the next chapter) but as an opportunity to push through, even when I didn't feel like pushing, to give it all I had, and to *grow*. As a result, I became more resilient, more adaptable, and a better competitor in life.

Even now there are tough days, those early mornings when I don't want to get up and get after it. What leads me through these moments is my continual return to those three questions:

1. Why do I do what I do? *Because I am committed to manifesting the goodness and greatness I believe is embedded within every human being.*

2. What do I want to accomplish? *I want to bring light and energy to a depleted world and help construct systems that optimize high performance.*

3. How do I want to be remembered? *As someone who loved Jesus, was committed to excellence in everything she did, and was relentless in her pursuit of true greatness.*

Again, this is what motivation is all about. And it is in those moments when we push ourselves past adversity or exhaustion, when we keep training or practicing or studying or preparing when we don't feel like doing it, that we really start getting good. Let's be honest: *anybody* can go at full tilt on days when they're functioning at 100 percent. That's easy in any profession or domain. But what makes a person truly *great* and how you get to excellence is to, at all times and in every situation, propel yourself toward high performance, even when you don't feel up to it. Give it your all, and give it your everything, whatever your "everything" happens to be at that moment.

Embrace the new. Push past the difficult by developing new mindsets, new patterned ways of thinking. High-performance athletes do this all the time; they can set their sights on how to be better, and then figure out how to get there. Retired NFL quarterback Alex Smith had a coach who helped him create this high-performance mindset by saying: "If what you want is different than what you have, then you need to change what you are doing."

Once we are open to developing new mindsets and enhanced levels of awareness and motivation, our lives, our vision, and our ultimate performance begin to change. Now, all of a sudden, our emotions, our energy, and our physiological responses are more in tune with *getting better, quicker.* Now we are able to position ourselves to become more adaptive and resilient.

When we return to the three essential questions whenever we need to reenergize, refocus, or propel ourselves (or sometimes even *force* ourselves) to that next level, we begin to tap into the depths of our own powerful motivational tools and resources. This is when we also begin to build strong, enduring motivation that allows us to optimize our performance throughout the highs and lows of any professional trajectory and, in a far more expansive sense, life in general.

We'll come back to these questions again at the end of this chapter as we'll use them as our Championship Mindset Training exercise. The hope is that you into the habit of using these questions as a guidepost—*beacon* might be the better word—to motivate you at all times and at every juncture.

Good, better, best. Never let it rest. Until your good is better and your better is best.

ST. JEROME

KEEP YOUR ENGINE RUNNING!

Like awareness (because, after all, motivation is a heightened form of awareness), we must constantly strengthen, nourish, and hone our motivation from the inside out. No one else can do it for us. And like a muscle that becomes stronger with repeated use, our ability to remain motivated becomes stronger and more developed the more we exercise it. It should be comforting to realize that this motivational energy flows through each and every one of us; it just requires purposeful effort on our part to tap into that energy. We've just got to do the work.

When I'm doing performance training that involves the development of motivational mindsets, I often the use this analogy: think of motivation as the fuel for an engine of a car. You can have the nicest car on the block with the most beautiful paint job, the most impeccable interior, the shiniest rims, and the fanciest tires. But what if your sleek, shiny, impeccably tricked-out ride is not fueled up? Well, you already know the answer to that question. If your engine is not in optimal working condition and is not properly fueled, it's not going to get you anywhere. You'll end up staying stuck in the driveway, unable to move even an inch. I see too many people who are just like this car example: they have so much potential for excellence but are deceived by thinking their external features are enough to get them where they want to go. But, there they sit, idle in the driveway of life because they aren't properly fueled.

The point is this: unless you're willing to put in the work from the *inside out*, and until you're ready to devote as much care and attention to fueling the engine of your car as you are to the superficial exterior enhancements, you're stuck in park. What good is having such a great looking car if it can't get you where you want to go? That answer is easy, too: it's no good at all. You'll be stuck in your own garage, and your ride to excellence and high performance will be permanently stalled. There are too many people with enormous potential sitting idly by in life because they don't know how to properly inject their motivational engine with compelling fuel—and I cannot bear that person to be *you*.

TYPES OF FUEL FOR YOUR ENGINE

While you could spend an entire graduate school career studying the different types of motivation and the theories that support them, I want to simply provide a brief, high-level overview of a few of the more common motivations. Being aware of these different types of motivation will help you explore even more intimately what actually fuels your engine. This deeper understanding will be to your strategic advantage, particularly in moments when you need to draw on motivation most.

External and extrinsic motivation. External motivators are things that drive you toward action and are outside of your being, such as a parent, a teacher, a coach, a boss, a deadline or anyone or anything that helps drive you toward your goals. Extrinsic motivators are the tangible rewards for doing what you do. They are things that incentivize you to act, such as a trophy, or fame, or a performance-based bonus. Either way, both types of motivation are outside of you.

Internal and intrinsic motivation. These motivators fuel you from inside your very soul. Internal motivators are the inner forces that urge you to continue growing, learning, and delivering your very best. Intrinsic motivators are the inherent value and deep satisfaction you find in the pursuit of your goals. Either way, both types of motivation come from inside of your being.

Social motivation. This motivator comes from being around others or on a team that is striving for a greater collective purpose. People with higher levels of social motivation are often those who find themselves committed to higher standards and greater effort while working out, studying, or executing a project when they are with other people, rather than alone.

So, on a scale of one to five, how would you rate yourself on each of these types of motivation? Understand that none of these are inherently better or worse than the other. What we know from a scientific standpoint, however, is that *internal and intrinsic motivations* are the longest lasting, most sustainable types of motivation we can cultivate in ourselves. (Hint: that's why our three critical motivation questions are so "critical!") We also know that while motivation that comes from outside of ourselves may be powerful in the moment, individuals can become exploited by those external and extrinsic motivations if they are not mindful: if we are only driven by others and chasing things like fame or money, there comes a time when we are no longer using the sport or the job for our own development—rather, the sport or job is using us. We find ourselves on the hamster wheel that psychologists call the "hedonic treadmill," which generates highs but never generates the type of meaningful, long-lasting impact in our general happiness or well-being.

Furthermore, while humans are social beings and wired for human connection, we can lose ourselves amidst the throng of others. What happens when the coach is no longer there, the crowd is no longer cheering, and your teammates are no longer around? If you have not cultivated some powerful, sustaining internal and intrinsic elements of motivation, it can be devastating and destabilizing. I wrote my doctoral dissertation on the topic of the transition out of the NFL. For those professional athletes who transitioned successfully, learning to rely on motivation from *the inside* was critical. So, yes, we can certainly use the other types of motivation . . . we just can't let those motives use us.

It is your job to motivate you. And hopefully, now you better understand some of the different types of motivational fuel you can use to give your engine a boost!

NEWS FLASH:
PERFECTION AND EXCELLENCE
ARE NOT THE SAME THING!

Whenever we are discussing the subject of motivation, it's important to keep this in mind, especially since societal norms want us to see it differently: **perfection and excellence are not the same thing**. In fact, far from it.

Perfection is unattainable. As human beings, we are simply unable to achieve it.

Excellence, on the other hand, is well within our reach. We were designed to be excellent, purposeful, highly disciplined in all our pursuits, and to hold ourselves to a high a standard of excellence. You see, excellence does not fear failure; rather, excellence allows failure to be part of the process. Excellence is not about avoiding failure; rather, it is about how quickly we can *recover* from failure, how effectively we can *redirect* when we misstep, and how successfully we can *reconfigure* our thinking and adjust our mindsets when we are faced with unanticipated setbacks.

---

*Whatever you do, work at it with all your heart, as
working for the Lord, not for men, since you know you
will receive an inheritance from the Lord as a reward.*

COLOSSIANS 3:23-24

Excellence, then, is about how we respond, how we recover, and how we think, at every level—physically, technically, tactically, mentally, emotionally, and spiritually. Navigating challenges and failure are part of the overall growth process. We will delve more deeply into how we can relate to (and grow from) failure as we examine the third play—confidence—but it is worth noting here that excellence, and our ability to constantly strive toward it, no matter what, is the underpinning of healthy motivation.

A MOTIVATIONAL MEMORY

I started playing soccer when I was seven years old. I loved everything about the game, even at that young age. As a junior in high school, I decided I wanted to attend the University of Notre Dame to play soccer. However, everyone around me told me it was impossible and I'd *never* be able to play on a team of that caliber because I was from a small town that no one had ever heard of and was on a club team that was not nationally ranked. They came up with just about every reason under the sun to convince me that I was not "Fighting Irish" material and that my dream, while admirable, was unattainable and unrealistic.

And then I heard Muhammad Ali's quote, and my entire trajectory shifted—and my trajectory shifted because my entire *mindset* shifted. Ali's quote reads:

> Impossible is just a big word thrown around by small men who find it easier to live in the world they've been given than to explore the power they have to change it. Impossible is not a fact. It's an opinion. Impossible is not a declaration. It's a dare. Impossible is potential. Impossible is temporary. Impossible is nothing.

I realize now, looking back, that I was given precisely what I needed to hear, precisely when I needed to hear it. And when I heard it, when I read Ali's quote out loud, I knew that "impossible" *was* nothing, and that if my going to Notre Dame was meant to be (and if I put in the hard work necessary to achieve it), it was going to happen.

So, I set my sights. I identified my goals. I did the work. I even got a rubber wristband that said, "IMPOSSIBLE IS NOTHING," and I wore that wristband every single day as I went about the task of preparing every aspect of my life to join the Fighting Irish. I was motivated to make it. To overcome the odds and do what I needed to do—what I *had* to do—to get there. And at the end of the day, guess what I learned? All you need is a simple apostrophe and a single space and suddenly "IMPOSSIBLE" becomes "I'M POSSIBLE."

So, a message can be a source of motivation. But the message must be internalized in a way that can motivate and propel a person to action. In my case, an apostrophe, an extra space, and high-octane fuel from within was what motivated me to make my dream a reality, even in the face of doubt and opposition.

As we prepare to examine the third play in this playbook, you should be able to feel the logical, sequential flow. These building blocks are not rigidly locked together, but they do *build upon* each other. Learning one play allows us to move to the next with greater ease and deeper sense of purpose and understanding simply because our awareness levels are being heightened at every stage and at every step.

We already know, for instance, that **awareness** sits at the center of everything, which is why this was our first play. Now we know that **motivation** propels us to a newer level of understanding and excellence where we are able to better understand our "why" and recognize what drives us. Now, as we move to **confidence**, we'll explore how to take this awareness and this drive and turn it into a dynamic that allows us to show up every day with self-assurance. This confidence is what you can step out onto the field with, what you can step into the boardroom with, and what you can wear wrapped around your shoulders when you step into every important moment in your life.

But before we step forward, let's stand still a moment longer to engage an exercise that will provide us the motivational fuel we need to constantly push toward performance excellence.

PLAY #2:
MOTIVATION

CHAMPIONSHIP MINDSET TRAINING:
"Critical Motivation Questions"

———

For this exercise, reflect on the critical motivation questions and write out your answers. Return to them often as you continue on this journey; ask yourself these questions whenever you feel like you need a motivational reset, jump-start, or simple reminder of your purpose, your goals, and your legacy.

1. **Why** do you do what you do? (purpose)

2. **What** do you want to accomplish? (goals)

3. **How** do you want to be remembered? (legacy)

CHAPTER THREE

PLAY #3:
CONFIDENCE

Confidence Is a Choice. Choose to Be Confident!

---

*Confidence comes not from always being right but
from not fearing to be wrong.*

PETER T. MCINTYRE

Sharpie markers became a staple in the football locker room when our student-athletes began to understand how to leverage "power statements" to drive consistent performance excellence. They'd toss them around the locker room as they each geared up through their own pre-game routine, writing simple words, phrases, and reminders on their cleats, armbands, or the tape that wrapped their wrists. They were cues: powerful, positive, productive statements about themselves, their team, or their mission. They were intentional and carefully crafted, chosen to be exactly what each individual needed to remind himself amidst the heat of battle who he was, why he was there, or what he intended to accomplish.

One of our guys had several power statements that were meaningful to him: words of power filled up the entirety of his taped, left wrist. He smiled as he wrote each word. Then he tossed the marker to his teammate and flipped his wrist over so I could see the underside. "That's my favorite," he said, pointing to a statement reading, "I'm a child of the King." I asked him what it meant to him, and his brown eyes stared directly into my soul as he answered, "Because this all matters to me and my family *so much*. And if I make a mistake, I know I can't lose my head. So, I just have to remind myself that I'm a child of the King, and that's even *more* important than football." And then, with smiling eyes and a boyish grin he quipped, "But you know, I'm also pretty good, Doc, so when I'm out there balling, it's a reminder that I best stay grounded, because while I'm a *child* of the King, I'm not THE King." And that's exactly what a power statement is intended to do: help us stay grounded, present, and confident in the moment!

*

External circumstances are real. They impact us. They change us. But they shouldn't control us. They don't have to derail who we are striving to become in this world. They don't have to wipe away our confidence for the next moment of our lives. And if we learn to *think right* about who we are and what we are doing (and have done), it changes how we show up. We can be propelled and powered by a confidence that comes from deep within us—a confidence that isn't tied to the outcome of the game or even on an upcoming performance, but is firmly rooted in who we are as *a person*. We are always striving for a win, but regardless of victory or defeat, our confidence level can remain consistently high if we learn how to build it in a grounded, sustainable manner that pursues excellence in the process and not solely the outcome.

Can you feel the progression and the interconnectedness of these plays? Awareness, the first building block, sits at the center of everything: **you must be aware before you can enhance**. Motivation, the second play, explores how this awareness makes us tick and drives us to do what we do; **you must understand your "why."** And now we are at the third play, where we examine how to **choose confidence every day,** in every situation.

The sad truth of the matter is that while many people are highly motivated, technically equipped, and deeply intent on becoming the next best version of themselves, they remain hesitant. Unsure. Doubtful. Unproductive thoughts and negative mindsets dominate their headspace and undermine their confidence. This takes us back to what we already know: **our thoughts affect our emotions, and our emotions affect our physiological responses, which ultimately drive our performance**. And when those thoughts become negative or unproductive, they can undercut (or potentially eradicate) our confidence.

Imagine wanting something so badly and even having the skills, the tools, and the knowledge at your disposal to get you there, but your own thoughts and emotions prevent you from fully delivering. Because your *confidence* is lacking, you're simply unable to reach that next level of performance excellence. This does not have to happen. There is an alternative. There is a clear choice here, a better way of being, and that choice lies within each and every one of us simply because confidence itself emanates from deep within. All you need to do is make the decision to tap into it . . . but this will also require that you do the work. This is exactly why knowing what confidence is, where it comes from, and how to sustain it is so vitally important. When it comes down it, then, remember this: confidence is just a thought; therefore, confidence is a choice.

My friend, colleague, and doctoral advisor, Dr. Rick "Coach" McGuire, would always tell us, "Confidence is just a thought. Since we can choose our thoughts, we can choose confidence. And I'd rather my athletes *always* choose confidence!" Just like the student-athlete who wrapped his wrists in power statements to remind him he was "a child of the King," you too must know who you are, at all times and in every situation. That young man knew precisely who he was beneath his jersey, just as anyone, in any profession or domain, can know themselves with just as much clarity and clear-sighted conviction. If you start with this essential truth, and if you keep your mindset positively directed, purpose-driven, and mission-focused, you are setting yourself up for success and stabilizing your confidence levels in a way that will make you better, stronger, faster, or whatever you need to be, whenever you need to be it! We are, all of us, blessed with this luxury of choice; this choice belongs to you and you alone. Given that vital and inspiring piece of knowledge, why *wouldn't* you choose confidence every time?

No one can make your feel inferior without your consent.

ELEANOR ROOSEVELT

CONFIDENCE CAN BE TAUGHT!?

I clearly remember sitting in my first applied sport psychology class. I remember when we began studying the chapter on confidence and how fascinated (and surprised!) I was by the realization that confidence could actually be *taught*. And, if confidence can be taught, it can (obviously) be *learned*! The revelation still feels as fresh and as vital today as it did back then, simply because it means that *anyone* can be confident; it can be deconstructed, analyzed, and applied not just in the classroom, but in life in general. Confidence is merely a mindset, a thought pattern.

Sitting in class that day, newly aware that confidence can actually be studied, trained, and acquired at will, it dawned on me how important applied sport psychology is to the larger world around us. Why? Because it helps us understand the nature of the human mind. It helps us figure out what makes us tick and keeps us ticking. And it allows us to manage and maximize our own performance. All of this speaks to **the transformative power of the mind**.

Even as a young girl, my confidence level was always fairly high. I was highly competitive, a strong student and athlete, and I was always willing to put in the work to become even better. Because I never struggled with confidence, I never gave much thought to its origin. In fact, I think I probably ascribed to the popular (and incorrect) notion that, when it came to confidence, either you had it or you didn't. It wasn't until that moment in class that I was able to wrap my head around the reality that perhaps the "it factor" could be trained, developed, and wired within a person . . . if they were willing to do the work and train their brain.

CONFIDENCE IS
"MONEY IN THE BANK"

I use this analogy whenever I'm training on confidence, because it sets up a pleasant premise: **I'm going to give you a million dollars**. Before you rush off to the bank, though, (or have the urge to spend it), consider this: it shouldn't be *a single* bank you're visiting . . . it should be *several*. Why? Because if you put all that money into a single bank and that bank gets robbed (and it is not insured), how much of that money would you have left? Zero. But if you distributed that money evenly by depositing $200,000 into five different banks, and just *one* of those banks gets robbed, you'd still have $800,000! And $800,000 is far preferable to zero, right?

This is precisely how we should look at confidence. We don't want to deposit all our confidence into any one area or into any single source because if that particular source is taken from us or is struggling on any given day, we have nowhere to turn. No backup. No reserves. Instead, we must fund our confidence across multiple sources so that if any one source gets low, we can simply draw our confidence from an alternative bank.

So, what are those different sources that can fund our confidence? We like to call them the five *keys of confidence*, and each needs to be constantly cultivated and continually honed. We need to issue "deposits" into every area consistently and with great intention to ensure they are never depleted, especially in moments when we need them most. Before we explore the five keys of confidence, however, let's look at how **confidence** and **performance** relate to each other. This is an important aspect of our foundational understanding of confidence itself.

THE PERFORMANCE CURVE
VS. THE CONFIDENCE CURVE

Everyone's *performance* curve fluctuates. We are human beings, so we will not always be at peak performance levels 100 percent of the time. The reality is that there are going to be highs and lows in the outcomes of our performance.

Our *confidence* curve, however, should not really fluctuate all that much. Why? Because confidence, as we've already said, is something we can manage and cultivate from *within*; its existence is not dependent upon anything but itself. It should flow through us in a steady stream, regardless of our performance outcomes. The chart below shows that the performance curve demonstrates considerable variability . . . yet the *confidence* curve remains, for the most part, steady and unwavering.

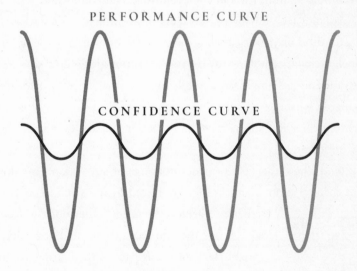

@Dr. Amber Selking, 2017

Figure 1: Performance Curve vs. Confidence Curve for High Performers

This chart will help us evaluate an essential question: How do we bring more stability to our confidence curve, even when our performance levels fluctuate?

High performers have a different relationship with confidence and performance than most people: a deeper, more holistic understanding. Their performance and confidence curves, while intricately interwoven, are independent, so you won't see any wild confidence fluctuations tied to the highs and lows of performance outcomes. If they're having an "off day" from a performance standpoint, for example, they've already trained their brains to separate their self-confidence from the outcome and proceed with courage and confidence into the next moment. They are even able to use this fluctuation in a way that will work to their benefit the next time around. That is to say, a bad performance does not create a downward spiral; rather, it's used to generate forward, upward momentum without compromising their confidence.

This holds true for high performers in *any* domain. They refuse to let a fumbled play, a weak balance sheet, or poor quarterly sales figures knock them off center. Again, because their confidence emanates from the inside out, it helps create a stabilizing force that keeps them focused, no matter what else is happening around them. This also quickens their recovery time and allows them to be better able to learn from their past mistakes.

If (and when) their performance does lag for any reason, they don't beat themselves up about it: they are fueled by it, driven to continue striving to achieve their goal. They don't welcome failure, but they do see setbacks and adversity as part of the process, as part of the journey toward performance excellence. This is the difference between being good and being great.

THE FIVE KEYS OF CONFIDENCE

Now that we have a foundational understanding of confidence itself, let's dive into the five keys. These are the five banks into which we must make our deposits consistently.

1. PAST PERFORMANCE

Of course, past performances are (and should be) an important component of confidence, but they cannot be the *only* component. As mentioned earlier, high performers in any domain know how to use *every* performance to their strategic advantage. The good performances they remember, visualize, and replicate. The bad performances they use as learning opportunities that provide critical information about how they can improve. It's simply informational, not emotional.

The good news here is that the ability to learn from our past performances—particularly "bad" performances—is not just reserved for elite athletes or for the highest-level "champions" in the boardroom or on the sales floor or in the classroom. The ability to learn from our past performances is *all* of ours for the taking. We just have to put in the work so we are prepared and trained. Remember that confidence is a mindset; it is a thought pattern, and so we can enhance it, direct it, and grow it at will!

The Best Way to F.A.I.L.

When it comes to mental conditioning and doing everything we can to stabilize our confidence curve (even in the face of bad performance), we must give new definition to the word F.A.I.L. We must now choose to see it as *First Attempt In Learning*. We learn from our failures, we regroup and analyze, then we keep on moving. Simple as that. Again, this is an acquired skill and a purposeful mindset that *all* of us can obtain! It is not reserved for just a privileged few.

I have the honor and privilege to serve as the Vice President of Leadership and Culture Development at Lippert, a global, publicly traded company that's been in existence since 1956 and is the leading supplier of engineered solutions to the recreational vehicle, marine, and other industries. While we have been in the game for decades and have core products and services that are excellent and enduring, there is a start-up mentality that still exists and drives our competitiveness on the margin. Here's what else distinguishes us from our competitors and allows us to showcase this excellence in a way few other companies can: *we are not afraid to fail.* We're obviously not out there *positioning* ourselves for failure, but neither are we bound or constricted by the fear of failure.

The company gets to excellence through iteration . . . *rapid* iterations that are evolutions of an idea, a product, or an inspiration. That "freedom to fail" is a purposeful acknowledgment (and a vital part of the company's overall culture and philosophy) that we are bold enough,

 brave enough, and confident enough to see whatever potential "failures" we do face as a way to grow. This does not unfold spontaneously or by happenstance; it is a culture that we cultivate, one that we are proud of, and one that puts us on the forefront of creativity, growth, and innovation. We are constantly giving ourselves room to grow. **No greatness was ever created by playing it safe**.

Remember the "Well, Better, Learned" Championship Mindset Training awareness exercise we explored at the end of Chapter One? It involves identifying, usually at the end of each day or event, three things that went well, two things that could possibly stand improvement, and one new thing that you learned about yourself. This is precisely why an evaluative exercise like this is such powerful mindset training: it helps strip away the emotionality that often comes with the highs and lows of performance, and it facilitates a more strategic approach to performance excellence.

We further the power of this CMT exercise by adding simple extensions that transform it into a strategy for analyzing performance:

1. What went well, *and why*?

2. What could go better, *and how*?

3. What did I learn about myself, *and why is that important*?

By asking ourselves "why" something went well, it allows us to pinpoint the reasoning, thereby allowing us to replicate those elements in the future. By asking ourselves "how" we intend to do something better the next time around, it allows us to put an action plan around the desired behavior change. And by asking ourselves why this is important to our identity, it allows us to develop a deeper understanding of who we are on the inside.

"Well, Better, Learned," then, is an exercise that can be used in any circumstance, under any condition. I have witnessed countless clients who begin using it for performance review and are suddenly able to see more clearly how to incrementally and continuously improve in their lives and work. They relish taking full ownership over the successes they have—not in an arrogant way, but in a *confident* way—in a manner that can be replicated. They stop feeling so ashamed of (and debilitated by) their past "poor" performances and begin, instead, to *own* those performances in a way that allows them to execute more productively in the future and move toward performance excellence from a more positive mindset. This drives them to feel a more grounded sense of self, a more purposeful sense of their own presence, as they navigate life.

The football team at Notre Dame used this mindset training exercise every Monday to analyze the game from the previous weekend. It brought such stability to our program simply because the players and the coaches knew what to expect when they sat down in meetings. Regardless if we won or lost, we reflected on the last game, closed that chapter, then realigned on the purpose and intent of the coming game each week.

The head coach conducted a full-team "Well, Better, Learned" exercise, and then coordinators broke it down another level for their units. Position coaches and student-athletes were also encouraged to do one for their individual positions and performances.

2. PREPARATION

There are four domains of preparation: physical, technical, tactical, and mental, and all of them are important.

Just as it is important to "distribute funds" to the different banks of confidence so that each of the five areas are addressed and properly filled, it's equally important to ensure that you're spending ample time honing and developing each of these four domains of preparation. Remember, performance excellence is a *process* and total preparation is always a part of it.

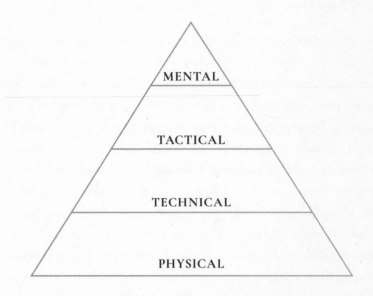

Adapted from Tudor Bompa, © Dr. Amber Selking, 2013

Figure 2: Domains of Preparation Pyramid

We already defined and described the importance of each of these domains of preparation in Brain Science 101 (if you decided to skip that part, I'd encourage you to revisit it!), so let's consider two practical examples of the importance of total preparation. First, do you remember walking into a classroom on exam day? If you hadn't adequately prepared, do you remember that anxiety in the pit of your stomach? Surely you remember the sweaty palms and the rapid heartbeat that ensued, because anxiety often manifests in a physiological response. But if you *had* prepared . . . if you'd actually put in the work and made the effort? Look out! Perhaps your prep looked like this: you'd gotten a great night's sleep and had a healthy breakfast (physical); you'd studied and had the facts clear (technical); you'd strategized on how long to spend on each section (tactical); and you'd developed a way to manage your mindset through the exam to remain calm and focused (mental). If it did, you walked into that classroom filled with confidence and clear-eyed certainty that you were going to be successful.

Here's the second example of how high levels of preparation will facilitate confidence. Many of the executives with whom I work on their mental performance have considerable anxiety when it comes to public speaking. This is problematic, since being an effective communicator is a vital skill to have in just about any domain, particularly with leaders, influencers, and high performers. We use the four domains to ensure they are fully prepared: we practice moving around the space where they are speaking and bringing the right energy for the communication at hand (physical); we ensure they have a solid outline for the communication, along with specific opening words, transitions, and closing remarks (technical); we discuss potential responses from the receivers of the communication so we can react appropriately (tactical); and we prepare a pre-talk routine, along with proper breathing, so he/she is in the right optimal zone for mental performance.

One of the effective ways to enhance your confidence level is by fully preparing for the task at hand. **Total preparation is key**. This is what I share with all my clients: **preparing intentionally and deliberately each day leads you to be physically strong, technically sound, tactically smart, and mentally tough**. So, the question becomes, why *wouldn't* you want to be fully prepared in all these domains?

3. SELF-TALK

Given that we have 70,000–80,000 thoughts per day, the thoughts you think and the things you say to yourself throughout each day are extremely important. Your thoughts, your mindsets, and your self-talk can either be confidence boosters or confidence *busters*. Remember that you have full control over these internal conversations, and also remember these conversations become mindsets that become patterned behavior. For this very reason, *the most important conversations you have every day are the conversations you have with yourself.*

The Power of a "Power Statement"

Think back to the football player I mentioned at the outset of this chapter and how the message on his wrist was a written affirmation and a powerful reminder of the person he actually is: "A Child of the King."

From my athletes, to my business leaders, to myself, we all have similar messages that we've woven into our lives. These simple, straightforward power statements remind us in one quick glance of who we are—not what we do or even what kind of athlete or leader we are, but who we are as humans—our *essential selves*. It's back to Brain Science 101: *Repeated thoughts build mindsets.* Mindsets are actual protein patterns that get wired into our brains and impact how we deliver in the moment. Power statements help us increase the predictability of wiring positive, powerful mindsets into how we operate along our journey toward performance excellence.

In a similar way, I had a favorite t-shirt when I was young that I wore *all* the time. It was an orange shirt with blue letters that said, "I am strong, powerful, equal, a threat." I didn't realize it then, because I obviously knew nothing about thought patterns and mental performance excellence as a nine-year-old, but I was already creating positive self-talk through power statements at that early age. Every time I would put that shirt on, I would think, *I am strong, powerful, equal, a threat; I am strong, powerful, equal, a threat.* Little did I know that every time I said that phrase, I was building a mindset—one that stuck with me and drove both my confidence and my performance. Even when our team was defeated or I'd be the one who got taken out in an aggressive slide tackle, I didn't leave the field sulking. Far from it: I left the field thinking—no, believing and *knowing*—that even in defeat, I was still strong, still powerful, every bit as equal as my opponents, and still very much of a threat. This is what allowed me to get back out there the next time, even stronger, more determined, and more confident. And this is how our thoughts (and, hence, our self-talk) can become wired into our brains and woven into our mindsets.

Years later, fresh out of undergraduate school, I found myself sitting around a boardroom table with a group of highly seasoned professionals (who all happened to be men). I made what I thought was a positive contribution to the conversation. Unfortunately, I was quickly rebuffed, dismissed, and demeaned by an older gentleman . . . who eventually ended up repeating my comment in his own words just a few minutes later! His comment was lauded and well-received by his colleagues.

As I sat in the meeting, I could feel myself getting smaller. I silently scolded myself, *Amber, couldn't you have kept your mouth shut? You're one month out of school!* That smallness and shame quickly evolved into anger, which eventually, because of the positive, confident mindset that had been ingrained in me since childhood, yielded to positive self-talk. I told myself, *Screw that! Remember you are strong, powerful, equal, a threat.* **I owned my own self-talk**. I did not let my thoughts run away from me, and I embraced the fact, as both knowledge and absolute truth, that I was strong, powerful, equal, and a threat. And perhaps this was just the reason why this man treated me the way he did. This is a perfect example of how important it is, when you reach a certain saturation or frustration level, to **stop listening to yourself and start** *talking* **to yourself!**

Believe in yourself! Have faith in your abilities!
Without a humble but reasonable confidence in your
own powers, you cannot be successful or happy.

NORMAN VINCENT PEALE

In addition to being mindful of and purposeful about how we communicate with ourselves, we need to be equally mindful of how we communicate *with others*. This is particularly true of group leaders, teachers, coaches, parents, company executives and managers—in fact, anyone in a position to lead, inspire, and motivate others. **Your words matter!** And the words of people in positions of power or influence simply matter even more. What you say and how you say it has a tremendous impact on the development of self-talk in *others,* especially with regard to young people or those who might already feel disenfranchised, disadvantaged, or in some way disconnected from the world around them (such as women and people of color, for example). Your words put you in a position of extraordinary responsibility; our role as leaders is a *big deal*. We should, therefore, always strive to develop positive patterns of self-talk in others, not negative ones. We must recognize the power we hold with every single word.

4. BODY LANGUAGE

Science tells us that our body language can either stimulate or drain our levels of confidence. The good news is that we have full control over our body language! The bad news is that if we aren't aware of this fact, our "non-verbal cues" (i.e., body language), can leave us vulnerable to an incredibly unstable confidence curve.

When we feel confident and at the very top of our game, we assume a "power posture": our head is up, our shoulders are back, our eye contact is direct and sustained, and our spine is straight. We're sending the signal to our brain that all is well, and that confidence is in the house! Such power postures can even trigger specific hormonal changes in the body. Remember that **the brain is always listening, always waiting for the appropriate signals**. The brain picks up on these postures and this mental messaging and, as a result, increases our levels of testosterone (the power hormone) and decreases our levels of cortisol (the stress hormone). The opposite is also true: the moment our head drops, shoulders slouch, or we retreat into ourselves to "become small," that same trigger alerts the brain that something may be wrong, which causes our power hormone to plummet and our stress hormone to spike. It's been shown that it takes as little as two minutes of a particular posture to impact hormonal changes! When it comes to body language, remember this: our non-verbal behaviors can strongly impact how we think and feel and, therefore, perform in the moment.

5. SUPPORT SYSTEM

All of us need social support and reinforcement. Each of us requires a support system that helps us process and analyze information, learn from our experiences, and shore up our confidence when we need it most. No one is an island. We live in this world together as independent individuals, yes, but we also live as interdependent human beings. Having a clear sense of who's in your corner, therefore, as well as a clear understanding of what role they play in your life, is an important way to enhance and sustain confidence.

Something else to recognize is that our support systems don't have to be *large*, necessarily, to be efficient and effective. I worked with a young man some time ago, a track athlete (sprinter), who told me he had no one in his support system. He never knew his dad and had recently lost his mom. He bounced around on friends' couches but never really let anyone matter too much to him. After we explored this in deeper detail, he shared with me that he *did* have God in his corner, which then created the opportunity for me to offer encouraging, supportive feedback. I told him that this divine presence was an important presence and that having a relationship with God would certainly constitute having a full corner! However, we also discussed the importance of learning to open up to trusted advisors as he sought to navigate this journey of life.

I love using boxing as an analogy when I consider the importance of a strong support system. During a fight, every boxer has a team in his or her corner that typically includes a trainer, a coach, an advisor, and maybe a parent, a significant other, or a good friend. Each person is there to provide a *specific type* of support. But when it comes right down to it, when it's time for that boxer to step into the center of the ring and face an opponent, he or she is fighting their own fight. That's how life is in a general sense as well. On a daily basis, we're all facing our own battles, doing the best we can, and trying to live our best lives. We step into the ring, and we fight. But when that bell rings and the round is over, the boxers retreat to their corners to seek the support they need from those who are standing there, whether it's medical attention, technical advice, or a motivational boost. This is the group that pushes the boxer and encourages continued excellence, driving him or her to continue "fighting the good fight." And if there's someone in that corner who doesn't bring value or vision to the process—or worse, who brings negative value or destabilizing energy—it's up to that boxer (just like it's up you) to move them out.

Just as important as knowing who's in your corner is knowing which person to turn to for specific resources at any given moment. If the boxer gets an eye injury from a strong right hook to the face, for example, they would be making a serious mistake to turn to anybody other than the trained medical professional for attention. *Knowing who to turn to is key.*

So, as you identify and refine your own support system, it's important to ask yourself these questions:

- Who, exactly, is *in* your corner?

- What are they doing to motivate, guide, and inspire you?

- Are they pushing you toward becoming the next best version of yourself, or are they inhibiting your growth?

- Are you taking steps to recruit the positive people you need and to remove the negative people that you do not?

All of these questions deserve careful reflection and sound, honest answers.

Knights of Your Roundtable

I spent some time with one of my friends, colleagues, and mental performance coaches of the Pittsburgh Pirates, who has his athletes engage in what he calls a "Knights of the Roundtable" exercise. The chairs of the roundtable are identified as different categories, such as physical support, tactical support, emotional support, spiritual support, relational support, professional development support—i.e., any support necessary to help keep athletes growing and developing toward their goals as a professional athlete but also (and most importantly) as a person.

He asks all the athletes to make a list of everyone who is a member of their support system. He then asks the athletes to assign each person to a seat at the roundtable, designated by the type of support they provide. Once completed, it becomes very clear to the athletes where the strengths are and where there are gaps in the support, which they need to fill if they are to continually grow into their greatness.

Who are the knights at *your* roundtable? Do they provide the kind of specialized and specific support you need in the moments when you need it most? Does their presence at your table have a positive and lasting impact? Where are the empty seats at your table, and what will you do to fill them? Consider using this exercise to help you take careful inventory of who's in your corner, and always remember that your corner should never be empty or lacking.

FROM CONFIDENCE TO INTENSITY MANAGEMENT

Now you have the knowledge and the tools to create, control, and sustain your confidence. Now you are poised, present, and fully committed to accomplishing whatever task is in front of you on any given day. But there could (and will) come a time when you're just not *feeling it*; when your confidence feels a little slippery and elusive. *That's not an excuse!*

Remember, again, that confidence is a *choice*. You've made the choice to be confident, and now you can use the five keys of confidence to eliminate the highs and the lows in a way that allows you to conquer your fears, navigate your doubts, and propel you toward excellence.

Now you're ready to move within your "optimal zone."

Let's learn what that zone is, how to get to into it, and how to stay there once you arrive. This is where *intensity management*—the fourth play—comes into the playbook. But before we move from this all-important third play of confidence, let's do a simple exercise that will help us generate and sustain that confidence when we need it most.

PLAY #3:
CONFIDENCE

CHAMPIONSHIP MINDSET TRAINING
"Power Statements"

———

In this exercise, develop three of your own power statements. Give it careful thought; try to closely examine which statements best capture and convey the essence of the person you really are or are striving to become. Keep them short and sweet. This way, they're easier to remember and also easy to jot down. Put them on a sticky note near your computer, post them on your bathroom mirror, or place them near the door as you're walking out to face the new day. Commit them to memory so that, in those moments when you need them most, all you'll have to do is draw from these new mindsets you will have wired into your brain through repetition.

You can use "I am" as a place to start your power statement, or craft something more universal, such as, "Leaders initiate contact."

I AM . . .

I AM . . .

I AM . . .

CHAPTER FOUR

PLAY #4:
INTENSITY MANAGEMENT

Find Your Optimal Zone!

Always work hard. Intensity clarifies. It creates not only momentum, but also the pressure you need to feel either friction, or fulfillment.

MARCUS BUCKINGHAM

Game day. The young athlete was set to start for the very first time as a football player for the University of Notre Dame. The stakes were high, the stadium was packed, and the adrenaline was already flowing.

We were playing against our archrival, USC. Thirty minutes to kick off.

As I stood on the field during warm-ups, I felt a strong hand grasp my arm. Big eyes peered down at me through his facemask. He was breathing incredibly hard, his chest rising and falling visibly under his shoulder pads. His nose was running and sweat was pouring off his body. "Doc!" he said, breathing heavily. "Do I have to be in my optimal zone right now?" Eyes wide, he longed for guidance in that critical moment before his first collegiate start on the biggest of stages. This was his moment, and he knew he had to get it right.

"No," I answered immediately. "Not until kick off."

"Then [heavy breath] I'm going to need your help, because I'm really jacked up right now!" he said, eyes still staring into mine. I put one hand on top of his shoulder pad and my other hand on his belly.

He tilted his head toward mine so I could speak into the earhole of his helmet as the stadium roared around us. His chest was thumping, and I could feel the adrenaline surging through his powerful body.

"*Breathe.* In through your nose . . . down into your belly . . . out through your mouth. Slow your exhale down. *Breathe.* In through your nose . . . down into your belly . . . out through your mouth," I repeated calmly, reminding him of the tactical breathing strategies he had learned in mental performance training.

Three rounds into the breathing cycle, I felt his heart rate start to slow. My hand on his stomach rose and fell less quickly as his breathing became more controlled. I spoke into his helmet the things I knew he needed to hear at that very moment. I reminded him of his goals, his purpose, his belief in his gifts, the man I knew that he was—the man under the jersey. I reminded him of how hard he'd worked and how much he'd given to get to this very moment. That physically, technically, tactically, and mentally he was a force to be reckoned with, on and off the field. In just a few moments in the middle of the field on that fall evening, this amazing young man found his zone. He quieted his spirit. He chose confidence. Then, he picked up his head, nodded at me with laser-like focus, extended his massive, gloved hand to give me a fist bump, and said, "Thanks, Doc. I *got* this." Thirty minutes later, he took the field, and that night was the powerful start of what would unfold into an excellent career at Notre Dame.

*

Intensity management is all about finding your optimal zone. It's about having your future hanging in the balance, then absolutely dominating that moment by bringing the very best of all you have to the stage. This is what separates the good from the great, the average from the champion, the one-and-done from the consistently excellent high performer.

Whether you're standing on a football field or in a boardroom or before the love of your life, **how you show up matters**, and you don't need to leave that to chance. You need to learn to identify, to manage, and to get into your optimal zone when it matters most! Knowing how to get to that zone quickly and consistently, and knowing how to switch to the right zone at the right time, will help you deliver the highest level of performance possible in that moment.

DIFFERENT TASKS REQUIRE DIFFERENT INTENSITY LEVELS

The more intensity you bring to a specific task, the better your performance will become . . . but only to a point. Your level of intensity must be appropriate for the task at hand. If you bring *too* much energy, if you're *too* amped up, your performance is going to decline, which means you are robbing yourself of the chance to put in an excellent performance. It also means that you're far more likely to miss both the moment and the mark.

Often, as in the example I used with the football player who found the precise level of intensity he needed at precisely the right moment, your "moment" might only present itself once. Getting it right at go-time is imperative. There is a direct relationship between intensity level and performance, and different tasks require different levels. Having an intimate understanding of this principle is vital if we are to achieve performance excellence on a consistent basis.

You can think of intensity levels as the physiological energy state that you bring into a moment.

In addition to being able to identify your optimal intensity zones (known as "arousal levels" in the sport psychology world) and knowing how to tap into and access them at any time, you must also know how to regulate and modulate these zones whenever necessary, and how to move comfortably between them as the situation warrants. Knowing how to "turn up" your intensity level when the task requires higher energy is just as important as knowing how to "turn down" when the task can be better accomplished with a lower intensity level. Delivering a speech to an audience of a thousand people will require a different level of energy and intensity than, say, having a conversation with your spouse. Driving a golf ball down the fairway requires a different level of intensity than putting. Stepping onto the sports field requires a different intensity than being in the classroom. **We've got to know how to manage our intensity and remain in control of it from start to finish to deliver the best performance possible**.

Remember that this is a *skill*. It's a learned behavior. And because we are capable of directing our thoughts and managing our mindsets, we're also capable of managing and directing our intensity levels. All of this is within our control! We should count all this as good news. Why? Because it means that all the mental plays and Championship Mindset Training exercises are ours for the taking. Managing your intensity level is a conscious decision; no one can make the decision except you. All of this comes back to *awareness*, that all-important first play from which all the others spring.

As we already know, being aware of our own awareness is what distinguishes us as human beings. That we are conscious of our own consciousness and able to make decisions about how to manage our mindsets and direct (and redirect) our thoughts are what make us uniquely human. **We have a choice.** Choosing the correct and appropriate intensity level in each moment is a choice, but as we already said, it is also an acquired skill; to do it, you must first *learn* it.

Your brain must be trained to step into your optimal zone (whatever that zone happens to be at the moment you need to execute) and to do it quickly and efficiently. Finding your optimal zone, then, is not a random occurrence. It will not just happen because you *want* it to. You've got to work (and sometimes fight) to get there.

Elite athletes have a very clear understanding of how and when their bodies perform their absolute best. They know what their optimal level of intensity is for each and every aspect of their performance, and they've trained themselves to be able to get into that zone on command. This gives them—as it will give you, once you master this important skill—the ability to perform consistently in the upper range of their ability, where excellence and even greatness live.

In a far more expansive sense, knowing how to micromanage your intensity level will also provide a stronger sense of control over every domain of your life, both personally and professionally, simply because you'll know what to bring to any given moment. Having a constant source of inner control over your energy and intensity is not only joyous but also *obtainable* for all of us.

SOME SCIENCE TO GROUND US

What we know from a scientific standpoint is that for every task there is a level of arousal or intensity required to facilitate optimal performance. This optimal zone, as we've said, varies from person to person and from task to task; each of us has our own "sweet spot." The good news is that each of us knows exactly what it *feels like* to be in our sweet spot! We know the sensation, the exhilarating rush, the amazing feeling of confidence and clarity that comes when we know we've got it *just right.*

The chart below is a variation of Yuri Hanin's (1978) Individual Zones of Optimal Functioning (IZOF) model, illustrating the relationship between intensity and performance.

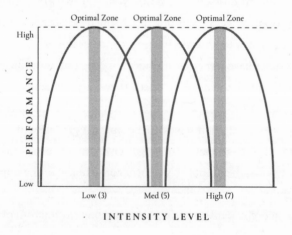

Figure 3: Intensity-Performance Model of Optimal Zones

The science is as clear as the chart. There is a direct relationship between intensity and performance, and knowing what level of intensity is required will enhance our ability to perform that task, and to perform it well. What this chart shows is that for any given person, on any given day, at any given moment, for any given task, there is an optimal intensity zone that will deliver optimal performance. Being able to identify *and get into* that zone is crucial.

You'll also recall another scientific concept we explored in Brain Science 101, which is that although the brain itself is not a muscle, it functions much like one because the parts we use most often are the parts that will become stronger. The same concept applies here. The more frequently you are able to get in (and stay in) your optimal zone, the stronger this skill will become, and the *easier* it will become. Why? Because now we're returning to the concept of **automaticity**, which we also explored in Brain Science 101. Over time, and with constant repetition, certain motions, skill patterns, and behaviors become automatic, which is when they move from our conscious mind to our subconscious mind. The same is true here. If we practice intensity management with regularity, it will become automatic. This is science-based knowledge, yes, but when it is utilized and applied correctly, it can tap directly into the limitless potential of the human spirit.

PUT A NUMBER ON IT

At the moment of execution, you always want to be in your optimal zone, whether that zone happens to be high, low, or somewhere in between. If you're bringing high energy to a situation or task that requires low-energy, you are not creating an optimal condition for high performance. What's important is not whether the level is high or low, but that it's **right**, meaning it's the zone that will help you deliver the highest level of performance in that moment.

This next exercise is one I use all the time. Think about an important task or situation where you need to execute at a high level; reflect on a time you were able to perform with precision and excellence. Now ask yourself what that moment of excellence *felt* like. What did it look like? What were you doing or not doing? Where was your intensity level at the moment of execution? Next, assign that energy level a number on a one to ten scale, with one being lowest and ten being highest. Remember that it doesn't matter whether that number is low or high; what matters is that it is the zone where you delivered your best. By giving a numerical value to your energy level, you will be able gauge not only where you need to be in order to execute, but also how far you need to go get there when that task or moment arises. Do you need to turn up or turn down to get into your zone? Know your number—your performance depends on it.

Knowing your "number" is also useful if you start to feel yourself slipping out of your optimal zone. When this happens, you can (if you're properly trained) utilize the tools you have at your disposal to get yourself back on track. Knowing what zone you're in and what zone you *need to be in* to perform the task to the best of your ability are two different pieces of knowledge. **Know both**.

Yes, all of this takes discipline and effort, at least initially. It is not easy or convenient, but what I say to the people with whom I work is this: **the pain of discipline is better than the pain of regret**. So, put in the effort. Develop the mindsets. Train your brain. Make the choice. Do the work.

Again, it's all about awareness. Remember that *we have to be aware before we can enhance.*

KNOW HOW AND WHEN TO SHIFT

I recently worked with a young professional who was required to interact frequently with both frontline team members and senior leaders from all different functional areas within his organization. My goal in working with him was to help him understand how to identify which precise energy level was required of him with these different groups and then how to shift into the appropriate energy levels given his audience and objectives.

Typically, senior-level leaders have many things going on in their minds; they move at a fairly fast pace, and their plates are usually pretty full. They are able to take in, assimilate, and analyze information and incoming data at a rapid rate. It's how their brains have become wired over time. The senior leaders this man needed to connect with would become quickly distracted (or even frustrated) when someone with a less intense energy level attempted to engage them at a slower tempo or in a less concise manner. Frontline team members and mid-level staffers tend to display lower levels of intensity (not *always*, of course). These are the people who might be trying to process or work through information at a more deliberate pace, or who are the do-ers of the tasks created by senior-level leaders.

This energy-difference dynamic can manifest itself in levels of organizational seniority, as we just mentioned, but often these energy differences appear between functional roles, such as engineering (lower) versus sales (higher). Different personality types can also reflect divergent energy levels in terms of how team members operate and execute. Of course, these are broad strokes of generalities, but you can see how these different variables can all interact and interplay to have people with very different optimal zones attempting to work together toward common objectives. What happens when that lower-energy employee attempts to communicate with the higher-energy employee? Lines are crossed. Vital information might be missed. Stress levels rise. Both parties walk away from the encounter feeling frustrated and misunderstood, simply because an appropriate convergence of energy could not be established. This is an avoidable circumstance. (Note: This is awareness of "dynamics," the fifth aspect of awareness at its finest.)

The young professional I worked with learned how to identify his optimal "number" when interacting with each different layer, function, and personality type of his organization, and he developed the skills he needed to remain in that range for long enough to ensure a successful outcome. He also learned to gauge and adapt to the energy level of others. Again, this is a *learned skill*. There are tools and resources available (such as Championship Mindset Training exercises) that can help you function at your best when you need it most, no matter what energy level you happen to be experiencing or needing in that moment.

It is important that you not only know and understand your optimal zones but also that you are able to communicate that zone to important people around you. Anyone with whom you come into contact can impact (often inadvertently) your ability to get into your zone effectively, and to be able to switch between and within your own zones as the moment dictates. For example, pre-game "pump-up speeches" may be helpful for higher optimal zone athletes but potentially disruptive for lower optimal zone athletes. It's ultimately your responsibility to get in your own zone, but having teammates and coaches around you who understand and respect what you need to get into your zone is always helpful!

*For a given person . . . on a given day . . . with a given
task . . . under a given set of circumstances . . . there is
a given level of arousal (intensity) that will allow for
an optimal performance.*

DR. RICK MCGUIRE

Now that we've explored the larger concepts and principles of
intensity management, let's turn our attention to some of the **tools
and strategies** that can help get you there. I use these techniques fre-
quently with people who need to perform consistently in the upper
range of their ability.

Some of these tools are designed to help you turn up your energy;
others, to turn it down. You'll see that several of these tools can work
equally well at moving your energy in *either* direction. What, when,
how, to what degree, and in which direction are the separate pieces that
create a single entity called Intensity Management. Being able to weave
all these threads together can mean the difference between mediocrity
and excellence.

WAYS TO TURN DOWN

TACTICAL BREATHING

Though breathing is one of the most basic human functions, most of us
don't do it correctly. The next time your intensity level is so high that it
prevents you from turning in an optimal performance, consider using

your breath to "turn down."

Let's go back to the simple breathing exercise I did with the football player on game day, just before he exploded onto the field and gave a performance that would change the trajectory of his career. This time, however, we're not standing on the field at a football game, we're standing in the middle of one of *your* most important moments, when the need to perform at a high level is critical, but your intensity level is off the charts.

Go ahead and visualize that place. Call up that moment in your mind. Remember the feelings and sensations you experienced that caused your pulse to quicken. Maybe you're standing backstage, waiting in the darkened wings, about to be introduced to an audience of a thousand people. Or maybe you're about to step into a meeting with your biggest client to close a new contract that's worth millions. Or maybe you're sitting down for an exam, or walking into a new school or job, or simply introducing yourself to someone for the first time.

Your breathing is fast and shallow. A trickle of sweat drips down your back. Perhaps your vision is constricted, and your hands are clammy or visibly shaking, which others will surely notice, which only increases your anxiety even more. Listen to my words again:

*"**Breathe.** In through your nose . . . down into your belly . . . out through your mouth. Slow your exhale down. Breathe. In through your nose . . . down into your belly . . . out through your mouth."*

Here's how to do it. Place one hand on your chest and one hand on your belly, and take a few deep breaths. Take note of which hand is moving as you inhale and exhale. Ideally, you want your belly hand to be moving out, rather than your chest hand moving up, because it means you're drawing the air down into the fullness of your lungs ("down into your belly" is what it feels like you are doing). This type of breathing helps increase the amount of oxygen into your bloodstream, slows the heart rate, helps release muscle tension, and helps you think more clearly and creatively. After a few minutes, we've actually reset our central nervous system. Science-based knowledge that enhances human performance!

VERBAL CUES (SELF-TALK)

You'll remember this from Chapter Three on confidence. Select a word or phrase that you can always turn to when you need it, to calm you down, help you focus (and refocus), and draw you back into the present moment. Write that word or phrase down, commit it to memory, and keep it close. *Let these cues become your commands: obey them when you need them most.*

VISUAL CUES

Quiet eye theory (Vickers, 1996) has demonstrated that having a specific focal point onto which you can narrow your vision for at least two or three seconds can help you quiet your mind, and connect the brain and body to improve aiming tasks, such as free throws in basketball or putts in golf. If we extrapolate this theory to apply toward optimal zone management, the idea is that you use that focal point to settle yourself down, lock into your optimal intensity level, and draw yourself back into the present moment. it can be something as simple as the corner of the picture frame on the wall, the water bottle in front of you, or a dot on your golf ball. Verbal cues can also serve as your visual cues if they are written in a prominent place where you can see them.

WAYS TO TURN UP

POWER BREATHING

These are strong, quick inhalations and exhalations, designed to turn up your energy and get the blood pumping. Let's say it's the beginning of the day, the very first meeting of the morning, and you're about to step into a crowded conference room to deliver an important presentation. The problem is you didn't sleep well the night before, so you're not yet fully awake, your concentration level is low, you're fighting off a headache, and you're nowhere near fully engaged.

 Take a minute or two to practice power breathing; it's a great way to find your focus, kick start your energy, and get you going. And remember: **just because it's an early-morning meeting and you didn't sleep well the night before doesn't mean you get a pass to be average**. There are no excuses for not showing up as your very best, giving 100 percent of whatever you have in your tank to give.

VERBAL CUES

Verbal cues can be just as effective at helping you turn *up* your energy as they can be at helping you turn it down. You already know by now that I have a favorite verbal cue of my own that I use all the time to help people find their focus, stimulate their energy, and turn it up: "LET'S GO!!!"

PHYSICAL MOVEMENT

This is a quick, simple way to turn it up. Jump around! Get moving! You see athletes doing warm-ups on the sidelines all the time, right? They're doing this not just to get their bodies and their muscles primed and ready but also to get their *minds* prepared, as well!

How do you get your own body moving in the morning? What steps do you take to stimulate, activate, and manage your energy? Focus more of your attention on this in the coming days and weeks and notice the qualitative difference and positive impact it will have in your daily life. **Remember that we are physical, mental, emotional, and spiritual beings**, so we need to activate and integrate all the different energy systems within us.

MUSIC

We all know that music can move us deeply, at every level. Why not use music as a strategic tool to either boost or lower your energy levels? Studies have shown that music is effective to help you turn up *or* turn down.

As we've already discussed, knowing *how* to turn up your intensity level is just as important as knowing *when* to do it. The method must match the moment. Put simply, if you're looking to elevate your energy, you wouldn't play a slow, sad love song, would you? Music helps generate energy, so you'd pump up the bass and maybe throw on some hip-hop or rap to put you in the right mindset.

FROM INTENSITY MANAGEMENT TO ATTENTIONAL CONTROL

So now we've explored the principles and practices that will help us manage our intensity in a way that will set us up for performance excellence. But before we move to the next building block of *Attentional Control* (knowing how to focus on the right things at the right time), let's do a Championship Mindset Training exercise that will solidify these intensity management principles in your own daily life.

PLAY #4:
INTENSITY MANAGEMENT

CHAMPIONSHIP MINDSET TRAINING:
"Find Your Zone!"

———

- *Identify* one or two areas in your own life where you really need to deliver your best in the moment. Then, for each area, identify what your optimal zone "number" is—that is, the optimal intensity level that delivers your highest possible performance level, with one being the lowest and ten being the highest. (Remember, it doesn't matter if your number is low, medium, or high; what matters is that it allows you to deliver your best!)

- *Practice* using one or more of the strategies we've explored in this chapter to help get you and keep you in your optimal zone for that task. Practice adjusting that number as necessary, to ensure you hit your mark at the precise moment you need to.

- *Be patient.* Remind yourself that this a process, a learned behavior, and mastering it might take a little time. Be gentle with yourself as you learn. Don't become frustrated if you miss your mark; just keep trying. With repeated effort, as you already know, your skills will become stronger and the process more efficient.

CHAPTER FIVE

PLAY #5:
ATTENTIONAL
CONTROL

You Give Power to What You Focus On

Distraction wastes our energy. Concentration restores it.

SHARON SALZBERG

My client was so excited about the new concept she had to share with her team, so I was thrilled to hear how the pitch went. Her deflated voice on the phone broke my heart as she recounted how she stammered and justified and poked holes in her own proposal, which ultimately landed the pitch flat.

"What were you thinking about?" I asked her.

"I was thinking about what *they* were thinking about," she responded. "And all the ways it could go wrong. Then, it did."

Just as I had surmised, she had allowed her thoughts to manifest into reality. She had given power to all the wrong things and left lifeless all the *good* things within her concepts and her work. Because she was distracted, she'd been knocked off center . . . and staying centered is the very essence of attentional control!

*

Just as intensity management is about finding your optimal zone at the right time for the right task, attentional control requires that same level of precision and intentionality. In the same way we can turn up or down our levels of intensity, we can learn to manage and maximize our focus as well.

There is a direct connection between these two building blocks. When it comes right down to it, both of them require "locking in" and placing ourselves squarely in the present moment. When we develop this skill, when we acquire this mindset with both our energy and our attention, we put ourselves on a path that will lead us to high-performance behavior that is sustained, meaningful, and repeatable.

Attentional control is all about being locked onto the right things at the right time. It is a purposeful process. By understanding some basic attentional concepts, you are better able to align yourself with the performance outcomes you desire. And although all the plays in this playbook are vitally important, getting *this one* right will optimize your life at every level and in every aspect. Finding your focus will allow you to be a better you. It is the game-changer: the driver of all things high performance.

If you noticed, there was a subtle shift in the energy beginning with our last chapter. The earlier building blocks emphasized individual elements of our human wiring, helping raise our awareness of our awareness, our motivations, and how we can create a more grounded confidence. Those first several plays got us here. And remember that we need to be aware before we can enhance. So, with intensity management and attentional control, we begin to weave these elements together in a far more integrative sense. Now we are learning to bring our energy and attention to the moment, as well. The first three mental plays got us to the right race; the next five help ensure that we run our race well and finish strong.

POWER LIVES WITHIN
THE PRESENT MOMENT

The purpose of attentional control is to bring our thoughts, our minds, and our bodies to the **present moment** to deliver high performance. The words "present moment" are operative: the moment we are experiencing *right now* is the only place we *can* wholly be.

Can you move into the past? Your body cannot, but your *mind* can. Recall an interesting conversation you might have had with a colleague or friend just last week, or remember an important point you made during last month's sales meeting. Being able to review, process, and analyze your past behavior or performance is an important learning tool. Revisiting the past in your mind can be a useful evaluative tool as well . . . as long as you don't wear out your welcome and stay there too long! This is when it can become problematic.

Can you step into the future? Obviously, our bodies cannot, but the future is where our hopes, our dreams, our goals, and our vision live. This, too, is a place where we want our minds to visit for a short stay to motivate us, inspire us, and help drive us toward the finish line. But it's not a place we want to call home. The future is not where we should be living.

If our mind is the past or in the future for too long, where is it *not*? The answer is easy: it is not in the present. And since we cannot be in more than one place at one time, since we cannot stand at the intersection of the past, the present, and the future simultaneously, we must stand in the one place that matters the most: the present. *Now* is all that we have.

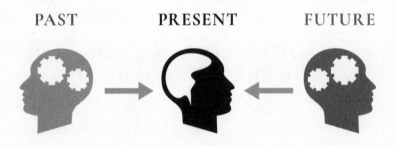

Figure 4: Cognitive Time Orientation for Optimal Brain-Body Connection

Knowing that we cannot be in more than one place at one time is itself an important focal point. When we talk about performance and execution, we have to learn to pull our minds from the past or the future into the present moment, because this is where performance happens! This mind-body connection is vital; it places us in the present squarely and securely. Here is where our focus should be, and the purpose of this chapter is to help you be able to do that on a more consistent basis.

SHIFTING AND INTENTIONALITY: THE POWERFUL DUO

In the previous chapter on intensity management, you'll remember we explored the importance of learning how to shift and maneuver between different levels of intensity as necessary. The same is true of attentional control. How do we shift our focus to precisely where it needs to be, precisely when it needs to be there?

These are easy enough concepts to write about and to discuss, but how do we ensure that we get there? How do we move from principle to practice when we're out there navigating in the real world, when performance excellence and achieving optimal results really count? What are the challenges and obstacles involved, and how do we blast through them to a place where high performance and even greatness live? How we train our brains to focus and to switch between different levels of focus will be explored in this chapter. Maneuverability is mandatory.

In addition to shifting, there is another important foundational concept about attentional control that we need to examine before we get to the actual tools and techniques: *Intentionality*. Being able to broaden or narrow your focus in the moment is not a spontaneous act. Knowing where and to what degree your focus should be applied doesn't happen on a whim or by the luck of the draw; there must be intention involved. There must be that driving, sustained desire within you to **own your moment** and to **lock in** when it's go-time. Mastering this mindset will generate a totally different state of learning, a totally different state of execution, and a totally different state of *being*.

Intentionality and the ability to switch from one level or domain to another are, like we already said, learned skills. This is purposeful behavior. And we already know that this all begins with awareness. It begins with your thoughts. You must *choose* them. You must claim them victoriously as your own. No one else can do this but you. Yes, I can *teach* you, but **you** must internalize, integrate, and execute.

When you stand at the intersection of intensity management and attentional control, when both have converged and can now coexist, miraculous things begin to unfold: your vision, your goals, and your perspective start to expand. You begin to see the world around you and your place within it with more clarity. This is where the highest levels of execution and performance excellence are happening, single moment by single moment. **This is where greatness lives.**

THE ENEMY IS DISTRACTION

What we need to keep in mind when it comes to attentional control is that the enemy is not the opposing team. The enemy is not your competition or the rainy day or the headache you have from staying out too late last night. No. As my friend, advisor, and legendary sport psychology practitioner Dr. Rick McGuire would say, "The enemy is distraction!" And it is a formidable opponent. But, when we know what we are fighting, it is much easier to do battle. This is why you must suit up with the armor you need to do battle with this enemy. And the first layer of armor, as we already know, is awareness. So, let's begin with some basic understandings about how attention works; then, we will move into ways to manage that attention to drive your excellence, moment by moment.

THE SCIENCE BEHIND IT

As with all the concepts in this book, there is some excellent science to underpin the magnitude and importance of attentional control. Wrapping our mind around these concepts allows us to integrate that understanding into our mental performance foundation and leads us closer to high-performance excellence.

BURNING MENTAL CALORIES

The brain itself only weighs two to three pounds, yet it uses nearly 20 percent of our body's energy! This is why students are often exhausted after taking a major test: they've not exerted their bodies, but they've exerted their *minds*. Being fully focused and completely engaged requires tremendous mental energy. This is why you must be strategic, and selective with what you give your attention to at all times.

MULTITASKING: THE MISNOMER

The brain can only focus on one thing at a time. When we understand the inefficiency of trying to consciously process two different things simultaneously at high levels of precision and efficiency, we also begin to understand that there's really no such thing as multitasking. Multitasking is a misnomer.

Yes, we can certainly *switch* between tasks, and many of us can do it so quickly and efficiently that it *feels* like we're performing these tasks simultaneously, but at any split millisecond the conscious mind can only focus on one thing.

Those of us who have built the mindset "I am a great multitasker" have fallen into the trap of believing that doing multiple things at once is actually more efficient and effective. However, every time we "switch" from one task to the other, and back, there is a cognitive residue that must be overcome before you can fully involve your brain in the next task at hand. *Constantly* switching can become problematic and exhausting because it burns unnecessary mental calories. Ultimately, this leads to inefficiency in cognitive processing and less accurate or excellent execution. Don't let that happen. Remain focused on the task at hand and perform it well. Then move on to the next one. *One thing at a time.*

LIMITED ATTENTIONAL CAPACITY

Our conscious brain has what is called a *limited attentional capacity.* It can only be filled with so much data and information before it reaches capacity and overflows. To help explain this concept, I often use an analogy of a 12-ounce cup: when your 12-ounce cup is full, what happens if you continue to pour liquid into it? It overflows, of course!

Finally, brethren, whatever is true, whatever is honorable, whatever is right, whatever is pure, whatever is lovely, whatever is of good repute, if there is any excellence and if anything is worthy of praise, dwell on these things. The things you have learned and received and heard and seen in me, practice these things, and the peace of God will be with you.

PHILIPPIANS 4:8-9

The above passage from the book of Philippians in the Bible has long been one of my favorites because it perfectly illustrates this fundamental theme to which I continually return:

Thoughts → *Emotions* → *Physiological Response* → *Performance*

When we dwell on the right things, on the excellent things, on the things that are worthy of praise, there is a sense of peace, of power, that will be with us, and our minds will move to a place of clarity, creativity, and courage. This drives our behavior, and, ultimately, our performance. It sets us up for success and leads us to performance excellence that is consistent and enduring. I love that this truth is also grounded in science and so can connect with *all* of us, regardless of our faith background.

Dwelling on that which is excellent is a principle—*and* a practice— that stands at the solid center of attentional control. Knowing that we should fill our minds with what is excellent has everything to do with not just how we perform a particular task but how we live our lives. And remember that excellence does not mean perfection: it is merely the absolute best of all you have in you.

Our cup analogy explains why it's so important to fill your brain with "whatever is true, whatever is honorable, whatever is right, and whatever is pure." If you only have a limited capacity, fill your cup with thoughts and emotions that are positive, healthy, and life-affirming. Make the conscious decision, the deliberate choice, to focus on these things, to fill your mind with the right stuff so that when the negative things like fear, anxiety, doubt, and shame try to get in, there won't be any room for them to enter! Conversely, if you do fill it with the *wrong* stuff—anything hateful, toxic, or unhealthy from sources that range from music to images to media—problems will arise when you reach your maximum capacity because when the good things like hope, confidence, joy, and peace try to get in, there will be no room left. The cup has already been filled. This is why we've got to be conscious about what we fix our minds upon and be **aware** that if we're filling it with negativity and darkness, we are leaving no room for positivity and light. The blessing here, of course, is that what you fill your beautiful brain with is up to you. It is a choice. *Own your cup.*

The knowledge that your mind has a limited attention capacity is helpful because it allows you become more strategic and thoughtful about where you place your focus.

So, before we move on, let's reflect on what we're learned by asking yourself a few questions:

- Am I filling my mind with the right things?

- Are these things in alignment with the person I am trying to be and the goals I am trying to accomplish?

- Am I setting myself up for success, for joy, and for excellent and extraordinary outcomes based on the things upon which I choose to focus?

THE POWER IS YOURS

"We give power to what we focus on." I wrote this chapter's subtitle to remind us, from the very outset, that we hold all kinds of power within us that we usually don't even realize that we possess. I selected the Philippians passage to remind us that if we focus on the *right* things, on things that are noble and right, we will begin to have a sense of peace. This is not just a passage, however, it is *a promise*, clearly stated: "And the peace of God will be with you."

This is a place where science and scripture converge and complement each other with perfect precision. We already know from our chapter on Brain Science 101 that repeated thoughts build protein patterns in the brain. These thoughts become mindsets, and these mindsets influence our behavior, our performance, and our overall outlook on (and approach to) life. So, wouldn't it stand to reason, then, that having an eternal peace within us is just about as good as it gets? And the way to obtain that peace is by focusing on those things that are positive and productive?

What we think about manifests in our body, often literally. Why? Because your thoughts impact your physiological response. For example, if you're standing outside thinking about how hot it is, it often seems to get *hotter,* and most likely, your internal body temperature has actually risen. Furthermore, if we're so busy thinking about our weaknesses, our insecurities, and all of the possible negative outcomes that might occur as we're about to execute an important task, we're actually giving *power* to those negative thoughts. We're breathing life into them. When I work with athletes who are preparing for a big game, for instance, I tell them, "Don't give your power away!" If they're thinking about the opponents and how fast they can run or how powerfully they can tackle, then that athlete has already lost. Choose to think a different way. Give power to the things that are positive. **Give power to the things that make you great, and those too will be brought to life**.

Always remember: your focus determines your reality.

GEORGE LUCAS

FRAMEWORKS TO MANAGE ATTENTION

With some basic understanding of how attention works for humans, we can now move into two workable frameworks that allow us to manage attention in powerful ways.

THE FOUR DOMAINS OF ATTENTIONAL CONTROL

The first framework comprises four domains of attentional control. Becoming familiar with these domains helps us better understand how attention works, how we can better control it, and how (and why) we can so often become distracted. Our *awareness* of these details is what will set up for success. Remember that we must be aware before we can enhance.

While there are four domains of attentional control, there are only two spectrums within which these domains live: broad to narrow, and internal to external, as illustrated on the next page.

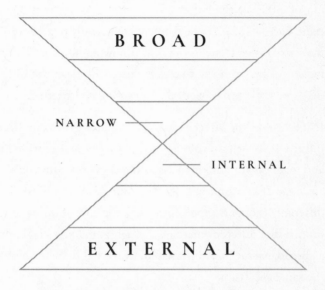

Adapted from Nideffer, 1976, ©Dr. Amber Selking, 2013

Figure 5: The Four Domains of Attention

- **BROAD**: When your attention is broadly placed, you're taking in large amounts of information. Your field of vision is wide. Think of this domain as you would a wide-angle camera lens: to get as broad a shot as you possibly can, you zoom out. You go wide. This is when your attention is diffused and spread across a large area.

- **NARROW:** The broad and narrow domains, while diametrically opposed, share the same spectrum. Think of the camera again. When you're looking for that tight shot and that narrow focus, you zoom in close. You're focusing on one or two specific features or details.

Knowing when to get into, when to stay in, and when to move out of either of these domains is crucial. A task that requires a tight, narrow focus at one moment could easily require a broader, more expansive focus in the next. Knowing how to comfortably maneuver between the two domains could mean the difference between sealing that big deal . . . or losing it altogether.

- **INTERNAL:** The internal domain is when we turn our attention inward. If you sprain your ankle, you turn your attention inward and focus on your ankle to assess the degree of pain you're experiencing. If you find yourself "in your head" rambling through different thoughts and options, your attention is directed inward in a different manner. Though as diametrically opposed as broad/narrow, the internal and external domains also share the same spectrum.

- **EXTERNAL:** Here is where you place your attention outside of yourself, to the world around you. This could be on a person, a book, or any external situation unfolding around you. Anything outside of yourself falls within the external domain. A certain task that might require internal focus is not going to be successfully executed if you're in an external domain. Being in the wrong domain at the wrong time can (and will) knock you off your game.

All four domains have an important function. What's tricky, sometimes, is figuring out the right combination and deciding which domain, or combination of domains from the two different spectrums, is the best to be in at the moment of execution. We all have tremendous amounts of data, material, and information flying at us on a near-constant basis. Knowing how to direct your attention to the relevant information at the right time will enhance your performance; it might even bump you from good to great. High achievers know how to lock into the right information within the right domain at all times, and if they're in the wrong domain, they know how to shift out of it quickly and decisively. **You can learn this, too.**

THREE LEVELS OF FOCUS

This second framework helps us understand the intensity with which we focus. On any given day, all of us move into and out of three levels of focus. Each of these levels are useful; each is important. None of them are inherently debilitating or destructing . . . unless we are not integrating and moving between them *intentionally*. When we get stuck and *stay* stuck, unable to switch or slide from one level to the next, we miss our mark—we miss the opportunity to execute at the highest possible level.

Level 1: Disengaged. This is when we are generally unfocused. Tapped out. Disengaged. There are moments when your mind *needs* to be at this level: even the highest performers cannot stay fully engaged and totally focused 100 percent of the time, nor should they even try! Brain-breaks like this are centering, anchoring, and mentally refueling . . . as long as the task at hand does not require something more.

Let's use the example of riding a bike. At this first level, we're just kind of rolling through the park at a leisurely pace. Nothing's in our way: the road is clear, the sun is bright, the sky is blue, and the path is straight. We are not fully engaged, just riding along, perhaps with our mind wandering elsewhere.

Level 2: Engaged. Our minds are more engaged with the task at hand at this level. Back to the biking example, perhaps it's a Saturday, and more families have arrived with their dogs and their blankets and their flying Frisbees. Now, we must engage our attention a little more, sit up a little straighter, and keep our hands closer to the brake in case we need to make a quick stop. We've successfully shifted into a level-two focus.

Level 3: Locked in. At this level, our focus is sharp. We are locked in. The park is behind us and terrain has just changed. You're in a bike race now, heading downhill fast. The path is now rocky and narrow; other bikers are in front of you, behind you, and beside you. Also, **there's a finish line, and your goal is to get there first**. Total focus is what you need now: you must be fully and completely locked in to the task at hand. And if you intend on winning this race, level three is precisely where you need to be.

What I see quite often with people, however, is that they might work very, very hard to make it to the finish line first (whether it's a race, or a sales pitch, or a big test), but when the moment is upon them and it's time to deliver and cross that finish line, they get distracted or pull back or stop short. They've worked so hard and then don't get the reward for it! Elite performers know when to shift into a level-three focus, and how to stay there all the way through completion of the task. *Then*, they shift down. This tells us something important: **you don't always have to be at level three. You only have to be there at the moment it counts the most!** And when you get there, don't let anything pull you away.

It takes an inordinate amount of energy to stay at level three. This is why I tell the athletes I work with to be sure to "lock in" at this level when it matters most. Many coaches and athletes demand this level of focus at all times, not always realizing how exhausting (and mentally inefficient) it is to be there when you don't really need to be. Be strategic with level three. Use it wisely in your life and in your work. But use it; too few people leave this level untapped in its potential.

The brain is designed to protect and preserve us. If it knows, for example, that it can execute a particular task at a level-two focus, it will automatically default to it to preserve energy and utilize its capacity wisely. But, if you've trained yourself to be aware of when and how to shift, it liberates you to freely flow and deliver your performance uninhibited by mental restraint.

HOW TO REFOCUS IN THREE SIMPLE STEPS

We are human. We all battle distraction. Sometimes we don't even realize we're being distracted: that's how easily it can slip in and take control. Consider this three-step process to help you manage distraction. You won't be at all surprised to learn that it all begins with **awareness**.

STEP 1: IDENTIFY

Identify the things that distract you and throw you off your game. Some people are more distracted by external things, while others are more distracted by internal things. Being aware of the distraction is what will allow you to *fight* it. Let's say you are easily distracted at work by things outside of yourself, such as whenever someone walks by your office. One easy fix would be to rearrange your office furniture so you're facing away from the door!

STEP 2: DECIDE

Decide what's important at that precise moment. Lou Holtz, the College Football Hall of Fame coach, calls it "The W.I.N. Principle," meaning "What's Important Now."

Understand that losing our focus from time to time is a normal part of life; it happens to all of us. But at the critical moment of distraction, being able to ask yourself, "What's important now?" is what will help draw you back into the present moment. And how you *answer* that question will steer you back to the place where your attention should be focused at that moment.

Consider the sales executive who's just had an awful meeting with her boss. Words were exchanged, performance was criticized, tempers flared a bit. Now, that same executive must walk into another meeting with a huge potential client with her focus knocked off center. By asking herself, "What's important now?"—as both a principle and a practice— the answer becomes clear: release that last interaction, and step into the next meeting with confidence and high energy, fully focused. She can (and definitely should) address her leader later. But now is *now*; don't let the past mess it up.

This is why W.I.N. is such an effective tool. In the heat of the moment, or in the midst of confusion or strife, or even if you're feeling just the slightest bit off balance, it allows you to recalibrate, refocus, and slide right back into the "home plate" of the present moment. In the midst of her own distractions, W.I.N. is what allowed this executive to push through that door with power and purpose, fully focused and engaged, bringing her A-game.

STEP 3: LOCK ON AND LOCK IN

This is where you've pushed through to get to the other side of distraction, and you've arrived at precisely where you need to be to execute your task with precision and focus. But once you're there, however, you've got to *stay* there. Don't get lazy or drop your guard. Remain locked on to the relevant information and locked in to the right domain and level of focus. Using visual and/or verbal cues is often helpful. Stay focused! Remember that this is a choice. It is a purposeful act.

LIFE IS BEAUTIFUL: CHERISH EVERY MOMENT

We now understand the value of staying in the present moment. This where truth lives; where greatness lives; where our ability to actualize and execute at the highest possible level lives. We must also understand, though, that every single moment we experience passes in the twinkling of an eye, and the moment . . . well, it's over forever. It is behind us. Before we know it, our moments have become memories.

This is why it's vitally important to still ourselves just long enough to experience (and yes, even cherish) every moment as it comes. We don't give ourselves enough time to be where we are. We feel the need to race through the present moment in a wild effort to make it to the next, sometimes without knowing what we'll even do once we get there. We've forgotten how to *feel*. When we're in pain, for instance, we try to rush through it. Avoid it. Ignore it. Similarly, we try to hurry ourselves through sadness, through discomfort, and through the dark periods of our lives. And the good times? We often we take them for granted and then wish we could return if only for a minute.

This may come as a surprise, but every moment, both the "bad" and the "good" have value simply because they are *ours*. All these instances form the texture of the fabric of our daily lives. So, let's try harder to remain in the purity of each moment as it arrives, without judging it, without ascribing value to it, and without rushing through it. Let's become more intentional, more purposeful in how we experience and embrace each moment, because we'll never get that moment back; it moves from a moment to a memory instantaneously.

As humans, we possess far more bandwidth than we give ourselves credit for; our capacity to experience the good and withstand the bad is boundless. Let's just slow down and *be in life*, not at the finish line necessarily, but wherever we happen to be in the present moment. We'll get to the finish line soon enough.

FROM ATTENTIONAL CONTROL TO EMOTIONAL MASTERY

Life can be an emotional roller coaster. And because so many people are driven by their emotions, they are often, unfortunately, unable to control or manage the direction and velocity of this roller coaster. It directs us; we do not direct it. But we don't have to be at the mercy of this wild ride. The choice is ours. The most effective way to master our emotions is by mastering our attentional control. And if we learn to identify and integrate our intensity *and* our attention levels, we align ourselves on a path that is good and true, excellent and sustainable.

Now that we know how to identify and master our energy and our attention, we are perfectly poised to learn how to master our *emotions*, the sixth play in our mental playbook. But before we jump in, let's try a Championship Mindset Training exercise that will help strengthen our attentional control.

PLAY #5:
ATTENTIONAL CONTROL

CHAMPIONSHIP MINDSET TRAINING:
"W.I.N."

———

Use the coming week to begin incorporating W.I.N. into your daily regimen.

- When you're facing a task that requires optimal execution and you feel like you're being distracted from delivering your best performance, ask yourself, "What's Important Now?" (Or, "What do I need to focus on at this *very moment*?") Let the answer to that question be the guide and director of your attention.

- When something goes particularly well in your life this week, you can still ask yourself another W.I.N. question: "Where must I place my focus to maintain this positive direction?" Remember that it is just as important to practice W.I.N. from a positive space! An athlete, for example, could make a huge play and stop his opponent right before the end zone. But if doesn't turn around and do it *again*, the opponent may still score a touchdown! Practicing W.I.N. keeps you executing at a high level on a consistent basis.

- Create visual reminders of your W.I.N. strategies. Write them down! Post them somewhere they can be easily seen—at your work station, on your treadmill, or even on your cleats. Train your brain to turn to W.I.N. when you need it most!

CHAPTER SIX

PLAY #6:
EMOTIONAL MASTERY

Control the Controllables

---

*Everything negative—pressure, challenges—
is all an opportunity for me to rise.*

KOBE BRYANT

We had already gingerly traversed four patches of late-season snow that remained on the sides of the mountain on our hike through Glacier National Park. While my husband, Aaron, and I enjoy hiking, I wouldn't consider us "hikers." So, as I looked up and over at our next segment of trail before we would finally summit the continental divide and saw that it included a narrow, winding, steep, rocky path *and* a snowpack clinging to the sixty-degree slope thousands of feet above the valley and lake below, my heart skipped a beat.

I felt my body flinch . . . my breathing became shallow . . . and my mind started to race with questions about what would happen if I or the love of my life in front of me made even one tiny misstep. We had come too far at this point, so I kept my thoughts and feelings to myself as we began navigating the first rock segment. By the time we got to the snow pass, I realized I had let my mind and emotions get away from me. My legs and arms were trembling from the adrenaline I let seep, unrestrained, through my body. I felt nauseous. I told my husband to go first as I tried to get my breathing under control and not look down. Once he crossed, I took my first two steps into the snow. Immediately, my body went into panic mode, and instead of allowing myself to traverse slowly and smoothly across the pass, I locked up; I bent my knees and leaned slightly left toward the mountainside, digging my bare fingers into the snow to balance myself. I paused for a moment, frozen in fear. After trying to take one step backward to get off the snow pass, I felt the snow shift under my feet and realized that would be even more dangerous. The only way to get out was to go through. Heart thumping and breath shallow, I took one hurried step after another, my fingers becoming numb as they acted as anchors in the snow. I felt myself somehow lock into a zone that helped me traverse the snow pass, and I made it across safely . . . but I certainly wouldn't call it pretty.

Once across, I wanted nothing to do with Aaron's attempt to console me and told him to just keep walking. I was mad. I was sad. I was all of the emotions. Basically, I was just *scared*. As a person who prides herself on handling stress and pressure well, and as one with very low anxiety in general, this was a rare moment in my life;

emotional panic is something I rarely experience. Once we finally summited the mountain, I was able to regroup with the help of my own mental coach: Aaron. He simply asked me, "What would you tell your athletes right now?" After I barked back some aggressive response, I knew that was the exact trigger question I needed. So, I took a deep breath, cleared my mind, and reminded myself of the importance of staying fluid, of trusting my gear, of breathing slowly. And then, I self-talked myself all the way back to the bottom of that mountain, across the same snow pass that nearly threw me off my game during our ascent. I used all of the mental tools I had in that moment—when it counted most—to make it down safely, because I would have been damned if I let my emotions ruin an incredible experience on a mountaintop in Montana.

*

It's been a while since I was in a situation so intense that I needed to exercise all the mental training I had to navigate the moment. But even amidst that experience, I knew that it was an opportunity to use my training; it was "game time." It was time to perform. Even as I was experiencing the fear and the rising panic, I was keenly aware that this was going to help forge something even deeper within me, and for that I was, and am, grateful.

However, very few of us see pressure as positive. We've been trained and conditioned to see pressure as more of an *adversary*—a destabilizing, destructive force that we must fight or a foreboding presence we must avoid. Our brains have been wired to see pressure as an unwelcome entity; a necessary evil on the battlefield of life.

But pressure does not have to be viewed in a negative light. We do not have to seek cover from it, nor must we knock it out with our strongest right hook whenever it arrives. In this chapter, we will learn to expand our vision and embrace a healthier, more holistic understanding of pressure. With the proper mental training, we can *learn* to view pressure as an asset rather than a liability.

Most of us are not on an actual battlefield (though if you are service personnel, thank you for your service and know that this chapter will assist you in the high-stakes conditions you face, too). Most of us are simply moving about in the world trying to live our best lives, striving toward excellence, learning from our mistakes, and developing the mental tools we need to become the best version of ourselves. This is a path and a journey, and at times, even a fight. But amid it all, we can learn to become the master of our emotions, thereby winning the battle within.

AS ALWAYS, THE CHOICE IS YOURS

Emotional mastery is learning to handle high-pressure situations as they unfold, play by play, case by case, across any and every domain, embracing each of these moments with confidence, grace, and enthusiasm. Pressure plays a role in this! So, let's use this chapter to redefine our relationship with pressure. **We have the opportunity as humans to change our perspective and to handle and process pressure completely differently**. We can *choose* to look at and relate to pressure in new and invigorating ways.

You can make the choice to become the master of your emotions. This decision belongs to you and you alone. We already know that it all begins with how we think about what we are thinking, and now that we are developing a deeper understanding of how these sequential building blocks work together to facilitate optimal performance, we can view and live life from a broader perspective. It is important to understand that pressure and stress aren't necessarily bad things in and of themselves: it's *how we view* them, and how we choose to process them, that will determine our ability to successfully navigate through high-stakes moments. The choice is ours.

Again, we can feel the momentum of these mental plays continuing to increase. We know that our heightened **awareness** is fundamental; we understand what **motivates** us to do what we do; we know the vital importance of investing in and cultivating our **confidence**; we know how to place our **intensity level** and **attention** precisely where they need to be, and how to step into and out of our optimal zones. All of these mental skills come from training, from practice, from repetition, and from reinforcement.

Eventually, as you transfer these newly learned skills from the pages of this book to the moments and minutes within your own daily life, you will move from an intellectual understanding of all of these principles to an understanding that is experiential and deeply personal. This is when the practical wisdom within these lessons will actually begin to *manifest*. And this is when you will be poised to actualize your own excellence!

No, you do not have to be held hostage to your emotions. Yes, you can give yourself permission to think differently about how you manage your emotions. No, this is not just motivational, feel-good messaging. Yes, this stuff is empirically rooted. Let's understand some of the science behind it.

THE PHYSIOLOGY OF STRESS

Once we understand how our bodies respond to and process stress on a biological level, and when we fully appreciate the physiology of what it *feels like* to be emotionally "out of control," we'll begin to better understand how to manage our thoughts and, therefore, our bodies in a way that optimizes our performance in stressful moments.

We already know, on a deeply intimate level, the physical manifestations of stress. Who amongst us hasn't felt the fluttering heart just before we deliver that major presentation or the can't-inhale-enough-breath sensation that might leave you feeling dizzy and disoriented in the moment before you take an important exam? You know these sensations because you've *experienced* them; still, let's review some of the most common physiological responses to stress:

- Increased heart rate

- Increased perspiration

- Butterflies in the stomach

- Shaking limbs and extremities

- Scattered thoughts

- The need to go to the bathroom

- Constricted vision

- Vomiting

All of these responses come from the brain, specifically from the **limbic system**. This is the emotional part of the brain; the part that allows you to react and respond to critical situations immediately, often without a moment's thought. Think about driving down a dark road and suddenly an animal runs directly into the path of your car. What happens? You automatically slam on the brakes and swerve for a near miss.

The limbic system controls your fight, flight, or freeze responses. Years ago, when more of our predators roamed the earth, this automatic response often meant the difference between life and death. It still does today for people in some situations, but in the domain of high performance, it's on a more sophisticated, nuanced level.

Being aware of the fact that this fight, flight, or freeze mechanism is necessary for our very survival is imperative, but so, also, is our awareness of the fact that this response should not be constantly engaged. This is not where we want to live all the time because the human body was not created to live in a constantly stressed, life-or-death state for extended periods.

The reality is, however, that our brains often trigger this mechanism when it simply *perceives* a threat. Perhaps it's when you're about to deliver a major presentation before the board, and you find you're perspiring through your shirt, your hands are trembling, and your lungs are unable to take in a steady breath. In this moment, you are not controlling your emotions; your emotions are controlling you, setting you up for a less than optimal performance. This doesn't have to happen! You can train your brain to manage these emotions so you show up standing tall, ready to fully execute and deliver . . . even in the midst of *feelings* of anxiety.

Many of the physiological responses associated with stress or high-pressure moments can be helpful and even lifesaving; they are vitally important *indicators* that your body is preparing you to respond at a heightened level. An increased heart rate, for example, means you're getting more blood and oxygen to your muscles so you'll be able to execute well in the coming moment, when optimal performance counts. Even vomiting or going to the bathroom means that your body is ridding itself of superfluous content in an effort to conserve every ounce of energy it will need to be able to execute at the highest level.

It's critical to know that you can perform extremely well, even if you *feel* out of sorts or anxious; it's all about how you choose to interpret the physiological response you're experiencing. Does it mean you're not prepared and you're going to fail? Or, does it mean that your body is simply preparing itself to be great and you must trust yourself in this moment? The choice always belongs to you, as does the control. This is what emotional mastery is all about.

The **logical** region of your brain (the prefrontal cortex) is responsible for thought analysis and behavioral regulation. Since we already know that our thoughts affect our emotions, and our emotions affect our physiological response, which ultimately drives our performance, we know that this is obviously an important part of the brain. The good news is that, like a muscle, the more we use this part of the brain, the stronger and more proficient it will become.

When we learn to balance, employ, and fully engage our brains at precisely the right moment, for precisely the right purpose, we have reached a level of emotional mastery. Tapping into both the emotional and the logical parts of our brain is a learned skill. As with all the mental plays, you must put in the work. Developing this mental maneuverability and emotional dexterity can mean the difference between being good and being *great*. And given the choice, who *wouldn't* choose greatness?

THE TWO SIDES OF STRESS

How and what we think about a situation or an event determine whether we see that event as positive, negative, or neutral. The choice is ours. The same holds true for how we see stress and pressure as well. While we are all well-acquainted with the overused word "stress," few of us are aware of the two different sides of stress. Let's examine them here, and let's make the purposeful decision to begin with the positive.

Eustress is *positive* stress, the type of stress that has a beneficial effect on our performance, on our motivation, on our confidence, and ultimately on our overall performance. Eustress is needed to help you grow as a human and as a performer; it's challenging work assignments or strength and conditioning training that help you grow. These are positive stressors that help you find your next layer of greatness.

Distress is *negative* stress that can lead to chronic illness, undermine your mental and emotional health, or compromise performance. While there are a significant number of negative, and sometimes downright *horrible*, things that are distressful, many of us have a tendency to create distress in our lives where eustress could actually be cultivated instead.

Interestingly, two different people could experience the same situation, but one may classify the experience as eustress and the other as distress; it all comes down to how they view it. When we say, "I'm stressed," we automatically assume that's a bad thing; I challenge you to consider which side of stress you're actually experiencing!

Cognitive restructuring occurs when you are able to challenge, replace, or modify a particular way of thinking, and it is most often used when trying to improve negative or destructive thoughts and mindsets. It is a purposeful practice designed to expand your vision, and a very powerful tool to have in your mental and emotional playbook. The end goal of cognitive restructuring is to replace distress-inducing or unproductive thinking with more positive, productive thoughts and mindsets. It is choosing to think differently, with a broader perspective, and refusing to allow one outlook (usually the more negative one) to dominate.

Now that you know the difference between eustress (positive stress) and distress (negative stress), let's consider an example of how we can use cognitive restructuring to generate more eustress in our lives.

As a woman in the very male-dominated spaces of sport and business, it would be very easy for me to create distress in my life every time I sat in a boardroom or a locker room if I *perceived* my presence was unwanted, not respected, or somehow inferior. But if I choose to restructure my thinking to believe in my heart that I bring a different perspective and, therefore, value to the team, that having a feminine touch in a masculine world is actually an advantage, and that any pushback I receive is because

 those around me are either ignorant or simply wrestling with the challenges before us as they would with any male counterpart, then I am able to show up differently. I show up more freely, more passionately, more determined to live out my purpose in this beautiful life.

TRIPLE C: CALM, COOL, AND COLLECTED

The goal, of course, is to reach a state of emotional mastery that allows us to remain *calm, cool, and collected*, even in the midst of the most stressful, pressure-packed moments. The challenge here is that our emotions often dominate and direct our behavior; they like to lead the charge, which is not a good thing. Because we allow our emotions to dominate, we often execute an act before we even think about it. When we allow our emotions to rule, we are the passengers rather than the drivers. At all times and in every moment, **we must drive the process**. We are at our best when we can employ the "Triple C" and stay calm, cool, and collected at will, under any given circumstance, for sustained periods.

This is what I tell athletes when we're learning the principles and practices of emotional mastery: "Great players make great plays because they've mastered their emotions. Nothing fazes them. They thrive in high-pressure moments." Now, this doesn't mean their heart isn't thumping, or the butterflies aren't fluttering around in their bellies, or they haven't had to go to the bathroom three times before they take to the field; it's just that they have learned to embrace the thudding, align the butterflies, and settle their bladder. They can't always control the physiological reactions, but they can control how they interpret and manage them through the art of *composure*.

You, too, can be a great player who executes great plays. Understanding the concepts of emotional mastery will allow you to redefine your relationship with pressure and stress and allow you to step off of the emotional roller coaster ride. But be patient. It takes time. As evidenced by my experience on the face of a mountain on that cool July day in Glacier National Park, we are ever learning, ever growing, ever striving to find new layers of our potential. It is a process.

THE THREE KEYS TO COMPOSURE

Composure, by definition, is the state of being calm and in control. These three strategies will help you master your emotions and drive performance excellence by maintaining composure in the heat of the moment. Learn to utilize and leverage these tools in a way that will consistently position you for success!

1. CONTROL THE CONTROLLABLES

This is a simple phrase that has become a verbal cue that reminds my clients of how to keep it together when things get tough or seemingly out of control. In stressful, high-pressure moments, you must identify what things you can control and what things you cannot. It's as simple as that. Unfortunately, though, *simple* does not always mean *easy*. This step requires clear-sighted honesty and the ability to make decisions soundly and swiftly. Although we should spend zero time, energy, and attention stressing about factors we cannot control, many people spend a large portion of their day in this headspace, and it's exhausting! Instead, we need to train ourselves to focus our time, energy, and attention on those things we *can* control. It is here that peace, poise, and perseverance reign. Remember, again, that this is a process: the more you practice, the easier it will become.

2. VIEW PRESSURE AS A PRIVILEGE

Every year, only two teams make the NFL Super Bowl; there are thirty other teams out there *wishing* they had the type of pressure the two final teams have upon them. For them, pressure is a privilege. Pressure is an indication that you have put in the work that has positioned you to be in a critical moment to perform; this principle is applicable in any domain. Instead of letting pressure crush or immobilize you, make the conscious decision—choose to choose—to view this pressure as an honor, a blessing, and an opportunity to deliver your very best self. There was actually a study done with professional cricket players that demonstrated that how they viewed the pressure of an at-bat had an impact on their batting percentage. Athletes who viewed the at-bat as an *opportunity* had a higher batting average than those who viewed it as a *threat*. How we perceive a situation will impact our how our bodies perform in the moment!

It's also worth noting that many extraordinary things in this world are made with pressure. How does a butterfly transform into the beautiful winged creature it is? By wrestling its way out of the cocoon. How is a diamond made? With tremendous amounts of pressure and heat. How does a high school basketball player become an elite athlete? By physical and mental conditioning, long hours of practice, and game after game after game of playing in critical moments. Human high performers have developed a more expansive definition of "pressure" so that it allows them to see pressure as an opportunity for growth and improvement. They *own* their pressure, and instead of allowing it to work against them, they *make it work for them*. You can do this, too. It all starts with awareness and with deciding to view every moment as an opportunity. Make each moment your own.

I might add that butterflies begin as caterpillars, diamonds begin as coal, and elite basketball players often go through an awkward, lanky season of life. Greatness isn't born; it's forged through a refinement process.

3. PRACTICE UNDER PRESSURE

We've already learned in earlier chapters that preparation is a driver of confidence. Practicing your craft until you can *feel* its nuances and its very texture will help ease your anxiety and bolster your confidence when it's time to walk onto whatever stage is before you. And since we spend far more time *practicing* for our big moments than we do *executing* them, we've got to make sure we find ways to create pressure within our practices. When you practice, remember to create unexpected bumps along the road. Create contingencies. Figure out how you will adjust if something goes wrong while you're in a practice mode; that way, you'll be primed and poised to perform at an optimal level when you're in competition mode. Get yourself ready, and at the moment of execution, *act like you've been there before*, because you have: during your practice.

FROM EMOTIONAL MASTERY TO MENTAL REHEARSAL

Now we can see a clear pattern developing, a momentum, with these plays in our playbook. The first three mental plays provide a basic, fundamental understanding about oneself. The next three focus on integrating these various elements into a more complete, holistic, and dynamic approach to your mental game. This next play is about weaving all of these elements together to ensure we show up, every time, in a place where we are physically, technically, tactically, and mentally ready to deliver our very best.

We have six of the eight building blocks in place for a solid mental performance foundation. Now, as we've come to master our emotions, we can bring each of them together into powerful *mental rehearsal* that will allow us to prepare in new, nuanced, and powerful ways for every single moment of our lives.

PLAY # 6:
EMOTIONAL MASTERY

CHAMPIONSHIP MINDSET TRAINING:
"Controlling Your Controllables"

- Identify three recurring situations in your life that are usually high pressure or stress inducing. What do those moments *feel* like? What physiological responses do they produce in your body?

- Draw two circles. In one circle, write down the things that are in your control during each particular moment. In the other circle, write down the things that are not in your control. **Think about purposefully directing your time, energy, and attention** to only the things inside your "controllable" circle. Leave the things in your "uncontrollable" circle alone . . . but be aware that they are there.

• Again, it is important to be gentle and patient with yourself; this is a process. The more you do this, the easier it will become, but it will probably feel difficult at first.

CONTROLLABLES   UNCONTROLLABLES

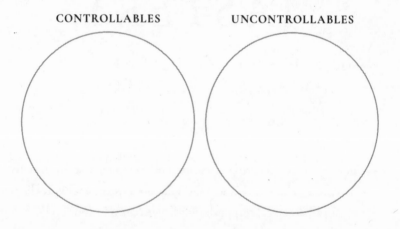

Figure 6: Controllables vs. Uncontrollables

CHAPTER SEVEN

PLAY #7: *MENTAL REHEARSAL*

What the Mind Conceives, the Body Achieves

Go through the game . . . The play is called.
See the ball snapped. See yourself carrying
*out the execution **perfectly**.*

LOU HOLTZ

"Well, *that* wasn't pretty," I told him as he jogged off the field after the drill at football practice. "Release and refocus. Give me one mental rep of you executing that play the *right* way. Don't let that last play be the last thing your brain sees."

He held my gaze and nodded. "Yes, ma'am," he answered, getting back into the drill line.

I saw him readjust his gloves, take a deep breath, drop down into his defensive back stance, and replay the moment in his mind, just as he learned to execute during mental performance training. He exhaled to signal he'd released that last play, then he tapped his helmet as a signal that he was refocused. And in that moment, I knew he'd rehearsed the play *correctly*; I was confident that his last neural "firing" was one of precision and excellence.

I watched his next rep. I watched his eyes focus on the right cues, his patience in his back pedal . . . and then his quick step into the trajectory of the ball thrown by the quarterback, all with laser-like concentration. His teammates cheered as he intercepted the ball, and he flashed a quick wink in my direction as he handed the ball back to the quarterbacks coach. This is what *mental rehearsal* is all about.

*

The first six chapters of this book have given you a solid understanding of how the brain works and how your thoughts, emotions, and body's responses have a direct, sustained impact on how you suit up and show up—not just how you show up to your profession, but how you show up for *life*. We've also explored ways to manage and maximize each of these first six mental plays in our playbook. Now, mental rehearsal will push us one powerful step forward in the process by allowing us to bring everything we've learned so far—all the tools and techniques, the practices and principles—*into the moment with us* in a way that prepares us to deliver our best with consistency and confidence. Mastering effective mental rehearsal gives us something else important, too; something that can spell the difference between good performance and great performance, and something that every high achiever seeks: *an edge.*

GROUNDED IN BRAIN-BASED SCIENCE

Mental rehearsal is one of the most researched topics in sport psychology, though these extraordinary principles can be comfortably integrated into any domain. To fully understand mental rehearsal, we need to go back to Brain Science 101, back to the underpinnings of mental performance itself and, indeed, to the underpinnings of this very book. It all begins with the brain. It all begins with our thoughts. And who controls our thoughts? We do!

What we know from a scientific standpoint is that mentally rehearsing a task causes your brain to fire in the same way, and in the same sequence, as when you physically execute the action. **The brain does not know the difference between what is real and what is imagined.** The *intensities* of the firing vary between what is real and what is imagined, but the neural pathways that are activated are precisely the same.

This knowledge is astounding and revelatory in itself . . . but there is more: mental repetitions are an effective way to prepare for a physical skill or an actual moment. We can utilize this science-based knowledge in a way that optimizes our performance, strengthens our overall game, and infuses us with a stronger sense of control and confidence in every aspect of our lives. It is within our power. All we must do is make the conscious decision to train our brains to become stronger and more efficient, just like we train our muscles. Think of mental rehearsal as a total body strength and conditioning training session!

Mental rehearsal, then, is far more than just motivation. It is far more than just visualization. This is brain training and body training—hardcore, science-based, neurological conditioning—that helps make us bigger, faster, stronger, and better able to deliver when the moment counts. This represents the mind-brain-body connection at its very best and at its highest level, and the power that flows from mastering this skill is virtually limitless. I have often heard the legendary former Notre Dame Football Coach Lou Holtz say, **"What the mind conceives, the body achieves."** Coach Holtz trained his athletes in mental rehearsal long before it was even a popular term, which helped elevate the Fighting Irish into one of the highest-performing teams in college football.

The brain is the engine that drives every aspect of mental rehearsal, though it is our ultimate performance that benefits from this practice. The good news is that, at this point in our learning process, we have acquired the tools and the building blocks we need to actualize and execute this exciting seventh play! We now stand poised at this new precipice, fully prepared to experience new heights and new levels of performance excellence . . . and mastering mental rehearsal is what will allow us to bring all of this together.

The "weaving together" process really begins in earnest *right here*, in this seventh mental play, and the way we do that is by learning to repeat and reinforce in our minds all that we've learned. We can mentally rehearse our *awareness* of all aspects within and around us; we can mentally rehearse reminding ourselves of our "why," which gives us another boost of *motivation* as we pursue our goals, despite pain or adversity; we can mentally rehearse choosing *confidence* with our self-talk and our body language; we can mentally rehearse placing ourselves in the *optimal zone* to deliver our best performance; we can mentally rehearse *focusing* on the right things at the right time; and we can mentally rehearse *mastering our emotions*, i.e., feeling calm, cool, and collected as we stand on the brink of that big moment. This is what mental rehearsal is all about, and this vital skill, once mastered, can and should integrate all the other mental plays into it. Again, this is *brain work* that requires training our brains to create the neural pathways we need to actualize and execute excellence consistently and with great intention. Remember, we must win in our mind first.

Every time you have a thought about an action, the brain sends an electrical signal, which travels through a series of neurons to execute that task. Every time you perform this action, it sends another signal in that same neural sequence. And, the more frequently you send that signal, the stronger the pathway becomes. This is how "talent" is developed at the neurological level, and this is precisely why mental rehearsal is an effective way to complement physical training. While most refer to this as "muscle memory," it is actually neuron memory. To illustrate the point with athletes, I tell them that every time your brain sends a signal to execute a task, a myelin sheath (as strong and as sticky as electrical tape) wraps around and connects those firing neurons. The more often you send these signals, the stronger this myelin sheath becomes. Just like electrical tape helps the electrical signal travel faster between two wires, so, too, does the myelin sheath allow the signal to travel more effectively and efficiently from neuron to neuron. From this principle emerges a simple yet powerful statement about how the brain works: **what fires together wires together**.

This is precisely why it's so important to make sure that whatever task you are rehearsing, you are rehearsing *correctly*. The last thing you want to do is rehearse (and reinforce) a task incorrectly. You don't want to create the wrong neuro pathways in your brain or body, so we must be mindful about what we are "wiring in." And, as always, be easy with yourself as you begin. Remember that this is an acquired skill; it takes time, energy, and attention to train your brain. It will not happen overnight. But also remember as you're learning that this is a purposeful process that must be executed with great intention. The brain is like a miraculous "muscle": let's utilize the tools we've been given to strengthen it!

As we already mentioned, what the mind conceives, the body can achieve. Consider this example: a basketball player might take one hundred free throws a day to hone his shot. But if he also *mentally rehearses* taking one hundred free throws in his mind, how many will he have taken in total? Here is the astounding answer: two hundred! Now, the mentally rehearsed free throws may be not as strong in neuro intensity for talent development as the physical act of practicing that shot,

 but they will definitely give him the edge he needs when it's game time because of the additional myelination it produces. And "the edge" is precisely what elite performers in any field are looking for when the moment of execution is upon them.

FIVE KEY ELEMENTS FOR POWERFUL MENTAL REHEARSAL

First and foremost, we call it "mental rehearsal" because it's just that: an actual *rehearsal* of the task(s) before us. While some refer to this mental skill as simply "visualization," that fails to fully reflect all that mental rehearsal encompasses. In the same way a dress rehearsal for a play runs through everything as it would be for opening night, so mental rehearsal should include every element of the real experience. There are five keys that allow the neuro activity of the rehearsal to most closely mimic that of actual skill execution. Each component is important to understand and to execute individually, of course, but much like these mental plays, it is when we can comfortably *integrate* these elements that we will be positioned to deliver our best.

1. PERSPECTIVE

Close your eyes. Quiet your mind. Imagine yourself doing three squats. Place yourself in that moment and complete all three squats. (Seriously, close your eyes and do this, it will help you understand what "perspective" is all about.) Now, let's go back. When you were doing those squats, were you outside of your body *watching yourself* do them? Or were you inside of your body, feeling the physical movement and experiencing the actual sensation of your body rising and lowering? How you visualized yourself in that moment will determine which perspective you used, because there are two: external and internal.

External perspective: If you were watching yourself from outside of your body, as a bystander, then you were using an external perspective. This perspective is particularly useful when you've already mastered the task and are simply wanting to create a quick burst of *confidence* before you walk into that important moment.

Internal perspective: If you were inside your body while you were mentally rehearsing these squats, you were using an internal perspective. This internal focus is especially helpful when learning a new skill or developing deeper expertise in your craft. This is the perspective that will build *competency;* it is also where your neural pathways are mirroring the physical activity most closely and, therefore, developing your actual talent.

As you become more practiced and proficient at mental rehearsal, you'll begin to see fairly quickly which perspective you tend to favor; this will be your **dominant perspective**. Neither perspective is right or wrong, but learning to move between them based on your performance needs will be key. If you need to build *confidence*, take an external perspective; if you need to build *competence*, take an internal perspective.

Say you're about to give a major sales presentation to an important customer, and you've practiced your presentation many times; you're ready to deliver, standing tall, and feeling confident. You arrive at the conference room early. You can use that time to take yourself through a few mental rehearsal reps. In this case, since you're comfortable with what you're going to present, it would be most beneficial to rehearse the scene from an *external perspective*, because all you need is that extra boost of confidence, that little performance push, to kick yourself into higher gear. This is precisely why being aware of the two perspectives is important, as is knowing which perspective to use under which conditions. Awareness stands at the center of everything.

2. VIVIDNESS

How do we make our mental rehearsals remarkably vivid? By employing all five senses, of course! If we've been blessed with the glorious gifts of sight, sound, touch, taste, and smell, why *wouldn't* we use whichever senses we have in a way that enhances our ability to show up confident, composed, and more in control, employing them in a way that optimizes every aspect of our physical, technical, tactical, and mental preparation for excellence?

Try this exercise.

- Recall a moment from your past that you remember executing to the best of your ability—a memory that was particularly satisfying and fulfilling. Take a few seconds to let this memory settle in around you. Take three deep breaths in through your nose, down into your belly, and out through your mouth. Try hard to stay in the very middle of this moment; close your eyes and put yourself in the center of it.

- Now, *in your mind*, open your eyes wide. What are two things you *see* in this moment? Engage your sense of sight and feel the profound blessing of being able to see this sight so clearly before you . . . even with your eyes closed! Keep yourself settled in the center of this moment. Take a long, careful look around in your mind and see what's there.

- Take two more deep breaths. Next, what are two things you *hear*? Listen carefully, intently, and with great purpose. These can be loud, dominant sounds or the subtler sounds that simply add texture, richness, and authenticity to the moment itself. Call these sounds up.

- Next, identify two things you can physically *touch* as you stand in the moment; perhaps it's your goalie gloves on your hands or your tie around your neck. Feel them with everything you have; focus on the *feel* of the textile.

- Take a few more deep breaths. Now, feel your taste buds actively engaging, preparing to receive the sensation of *taste*. Open your mouth slightly. What are two things that you taste in this magnificent moment of yours? Let those tastes play on your tongue; savor them.

- Keep breathing deeply in and out and, as you fill your lungs, allow your brain to activate your sense of *smell*. What scents are coming in with this oxygen you're inhaling? Let the smells fill you up.

The goal of this exercise is to make the moment *and* the memory feel as real as possible. Remember, the more vivid the mental rehearsal, the closer your brain will come to duplicating these neural pathways so they are firing precisely as they would while executing the actual activity. This is brain work, and it takes energy and effort. Make the decision to put in the work . . . then put in the work!

A Powerful Practice and Vivid Visual

Professional baseball is known for having some of the most advanced mental performance training systems of all sports. One of my colleagues is a mental performance coach for one of the teams and shared with me some of the mental training techniques that worked particularly well with their team. During practice, the players were asked to focus on a different sense every day. During the first day, they were to focus on sight: what were they seeing out on the field? They were to focus on these visual elements in vivid detail: the sight of the ball coming toward them, the height of the pitcher's mound, the grooves and crevices of their leather mitts. That evening, they were to mentally rehearse and carefully review of all those things, devoting fifteen to twenty minutes to replaying those sights in their minds as vividly as possible. As they did, they were training their brains to be able to vividly use their mind's eye.

The next day, they were required to focus on what they *heard* out on the field: the sound of the bat hitting the ball, the sound of their pounding footsteps as they rounded the bases, and so on. That evening, they did some more mental rehearsal, focusing on sounds *and* the sights, integrating the senses together.

Each day and each evening for five days, they employed each one of their senses, not just during the physical practice but also in the evening, during their mental rehearsals. This allowed them to recall and remember all the things they did right throughout the week in extreme detail so that when game day arrived, they could bring it all back and execute what they had mentally rehearsed.

It's worth noting that the team went to the World Series that year!

I always visualize the run before I do it. By the time I get to the start gate, I've run that race a hundred times already in my head, picturing how I'll take the turns.

LINDSEY VONN

---

3. CONTROL

During mental rehearsal, we always want to see the *right things. Never rehearse yourself making an error.* You want to make sure you are myelinating the *right* neuropathways and controlling the image you are allowing to replay in your mind. If you do want to practice how you will *respond* to an error, I always advise clients to drop themselves into the moment immediately *after* they've made the mistake and then rehearse making the necessary adaptations to recover correctly. During my days as a soccer player, let's say I lost the ball. I didn't want to mentally rehearse myself *losing the ball.* Those are not the neural pathways I wanted to establish. If I wanted to practice responding to adverse situations, I needed to focus mental energy on what I should do right *after* I lost the ball to correct the action and get myself (and my team) back on track. Mentally rehearse executing a task the right way . . . never the wrong way.

Pre-Game Rehearsal

When I'm working with clients on mastering mental rehearsal, I often share the example of a hockey goalie I worked with for years who has an extensive pre-game routine that powerfully integrates mental rehearsal. Hours before the puck drops, he suits up in *full gear*, skates onto the ice, and positions himself in front of the goal. He then rehearses segments of the game in his head, running through plays, in an empty arena! He visualizes his opponents skating toward him, shooting in stride. He imagines the sound of the blades crunching through the ice, the puck's trajectory as it travels toward him upwards of 100 mph, and most importantly, he visualizes himself *stopping* the puck. He sees himself and *feels* himself doing whatever it takes to stop the puck, offering his entire body as a sacrifice and, at the last moment, sticking his glove out for what would have been a sure goal. Even the rising swell of the cheering crowd as he helps lead his team to victory is part of this moment. This is mental rehearsal at its finest.

This example also underscores the fact that mental rehearsal doesn't have to be practiced with your eyes closed and with soft music playing in the background. *Feel* that hockey stick in your hands! *See* that puck coming straight at you! *Hear* that crowd roaring in anticipation as you execute that ultimate move and block that goal . . . and win that game! The more vivid the rehearsal, the better your brain can mirror the image. Make the moment count!

4. TIMING AND PACE

Mentally rehearsing a specific task with the appropriate timing and at the right pace is vital. If you are just learning a skill, you should slow it down in your mind to ensure you are integrating each critical nuance; this is when it becomes useful to rehearse the skill *slowly* in your mind. Take your time and let it fully play out, as if you were part of a slow-motion film. As you grow in your competence of the skill, task, or sequence at hand, rehearse the act in real time, just as you would if you were executing it in the moment. This will ensure that you are firing the neural pathways at the right tempo for whatever action you need to execute.

A Miraculous Mind-Body Connection

Here is a perfect example of how elite performers utilize timing and pace in their mental rehearsals to great benefit. Again, this is what helps give them the **edge**. A fascinating mental rehearsal study was performed with a group of Olympic track athletes. Each athlete was connected to a brain scanning device, given a timer to hold, and then instructed to run their race *in their minds*, starting and stopping their timers at the outset of the race and at the moment they crossed the finish line. What unfolded? Their times were the same as their normal speeds, as if they were racing on the actual track! This perfectly illustrates the fact that it is possible to use pace, timing, perspective, and vividness so effectively during mental rehearsal that it creates the same results as if you were performing the physical task. The good news here is that you don't have to be an Olympic athlete to achieve this degree of proficiency—just totally committed to the process itself. You must own the process completely.

5. REPETITION

This element speaks for itself, and we've spoken of it throughout the course of this book. The more frequently you repeat a task, the more proficient you will become at it. The exact same principle holds true in mental rehearsal. The more you practice the technique, the better you'll become . . . not just at the act of mental rehearsal, but at the task itself that you are mentally rehearsing. I spent two summers working at IMG Academy as a mental conditioning coach, where a well-known track athlete became so proficient at mental rehearsal he'd actually *break a sweat* as he was running the 400-meter race in his mind! That's how good he got at controlling every single aspect of his mental activity with an internal perspective, amazing vividness, and at precise timing and pace.

Hold a picture of yourself long and steadily enough in your mind's eye, and you will be drawn to it.

NAPOLEON HILL

FIVE Cs: CONCENTRATION, CONTROL, CONFIDENCE, COMPETENCE, AND COMPOSURE

Mental rehearsal is not just a skill reserved for elite athletes. It's not only reserved for high achievers. No matter where you are on the performance scale, and regardless of your profession or domain, you can use mental rehearsal to improve. To become stronger, faster, *better*. If you're just starting out, you can get good. If you're good, you can become great. If you're great, you can become consistently excellent.

Again, we call it mental rehearsal because it should be like the dress rehearsal of a play: all the lights, all the costumes, all the lines, all the emotions. It is a full run-through with every element engaged. Bring your moment to life in your mind. Incorporate all the other mental plays into your "script," where you employ proper breathing at just the right moments, where you use your visual and verbal cues to lock in at precisely the right time, where you dial into your optimal zone, and where feel your full self coming into and executing in that moment. By focusing your time, attention, and effort on mastering mental rehearsal, **these five Cs**—concentration, control, confidence, competence, and composure—can be yours. But the *decision* is yours, too. To get what you want, you have to be willing to do what it takes to get it. Mental rehearsal can be a bridge to help you get to your destination, but you must choose to cross it.

FROM MENTAL REHEARSAL TO ROUTINES

While mental rehearsal allows us to bring the first six plays into the moment to gain the critical edge that can mean the difference between being good and being great, the eighth and final mental play we're about to examine will allow us to **build routines** around these critical moments. These routines will help us set important patterns throughout the day, prepare us to deliver our very best, and allow us to regroup and recover throughout the course of the day. But before we get to our last play, let's get to this Championship Mindset Training exercise for mental rehearsal.

PLAY #7:
MENTAL REHEARSAL

CHAMPIONSHIP MINDSET TRAINING:
"5 Minutes, 5 Senses"

———

- Close your eyes, slow your breathing, and settle into one of your favorite memories. It can be an event from as far back as your childhood or a defining moment you might have experienced last week. Find that moment and settle in its midst. Do not rush. It sometimes takes a few minutes to find it and stand solidly at its center. Be patient with yourself during this process.

- Now that you're in it, employ each of your five senses so that you are able to bring it to life. Visualize the sights. Call up the sounds. Remember the touch. Activate your taste buds. Breathe in deeply and recall the smells. Writing them down might help enhance their clarity, at least until you become accustomed to this process. Stay in this moment for *five minutes*. This is, in fact, a long time (perhaps longer than the original moment lasted!), but it will allow you to fully focus on each sensory experience (one minute each).

- Try it for five days. Five minutes, for five days, using your five senses. This will train your brain to create vivid and, therefore, powerful mental rehearsals.

- Once you begin feeling more proficient at mental rehearsal, start using it as a preparation strategy before meetings, games, interviews, and so on.

CHAPTER EIGHT

PLAY #8:
ROUTINES

How You Do Anything Is How You Do Everything

> *Moral excellence comes about as a result of habit.*
> *We become just by doing just acts; temperate by doing*
> *temperate acts; brave by doing brave acts.*
>
> ARISTOTLE

I had a client who loved selling. But, dang! The amount of "No's" or "Not yets" he received throughout the day wore on him. He shared that his first meeting always set the tone for the rest of his day, so he really tried to ensure success in that initial interaction; otherwise, he was in a funk for the rest of the day. When I asked him how that was working out for him, he shrugged his shoulders and laughed, "I mean, it's sales—you can't win them all."

He seemed resigned to the notion that his persistent negative mindset that lingered after an unsuccessful interaction was just part of the process. I challenged him with my belief that it didn't *have* to be that way; that one unsuccessful moment didn't need to compound into an entire day of mediocrity if he simply disciplined his mind and approached selling in a more strategic and intentional way.

He, like most salespeople with whom I work, had a fairly decent morning routine: he woke up at a consistent time every morning, worked out, and then listened to podcasts on his way to work. But from there, it got a little hazy. So, we looked at building specific routines for *between* meetings; consistent ways that he could reset and refocus, interaction by interaction. His routine was simple: inhale deeply to absorb the moment, exhale to release the last interaction and slow his heart rate, mentally rehearse exactly how he wanted that next meeting to unfold, say his power statement to help reset his confidence and find his optimal zone, and remind himself why he was working so hard in the first place.

As time went on, he began to notice how much more stable his days felt, how his first interaction didn't determine the tone for the entire day, and how much more control he felt over the highs *and* the lows that he experienced. And then we started establishing his *post*-work routine. Instead of walking into the house with his phone still attached to his ear and feeling overwhelmed, he set a new routine of simply focusing on his breathing for two minutes in his car prior to entering the house. He also built specific, short windows of work time into his evenings, which helped to ensure he was fully present with his family. It felt more satisfying to walk into his home feeling like he was controlling his work versus it controlling him, ready to embrace his elated three-year-old son yelling, "Daddy! Daddy! Daddy!" and kiss his beautiful wife, who'd also just returned home from a long day at work. This is the power of routines.

*

Though this is the final mental play, this is the first time we are able to examine all eight plays from a fully integrated perspective that weaves all of these sequenced threads into a beautiful tapestry of high-performance excellence.

Now we are able to look back and appreciate the individuality and value of each of the previous plays while also embracing the final one (the importance of developing *healthy routines*) in a way that brings the entire picture into full focus. Now we can look at Championship Mindset Training, and excellence itself, through a prism of full and glorious color. Our vision has expanded.

We know these plays are sequential. There is purpose, intention, and strategic precision behind my design of this foundational mental performance training program. Now you can reflect and fully absorb these individual and collective principles at an intellectual level . . . but you can also move forward to activate and execute these concepts on an experiential level! **Your vision has not only been widened; it has been *sharpened*,** and your ability to build effective routines into your daily life, moment by moment, will be what reinforces all the tools you now have in your possession—tools that will nurture and facilitate a high-performance mindset and build the habits of excellence necessary for you to reach the next layer of your greatness.

The first six plays were conceptual in nature, with pragmatic approaches to developing them as skills. These final two plays of **mental rehearsal** and **routines** are focused more on putting the pieces together to formulate holistic and consistent methods for achieving high performance. Positive mindsets and purposeful actions will drive us toward excellence. And what have we said throughout the course of this book? **We choose our thoughts and build our mindsets**; no one else can do this for us.

This awareness of the power of choice is even more energizing *now* as we draw near to the book's conclusion than it was when we first explored this concept at the very outset. Why? Because now that we are fully outfitted with the tools we need to embark on this journey toward excellence, we can give ourselves permission to make the right choices at the right moments.

Before we dive into the power of habits and the importance of routines to help us build those habits, though, I want to return to another recurring theme we've explored in previous chapters: **intentionality and purpose**. These concepts, too, will unify and integrate everything we've learned so far in a way that positions us to embrace all eight of these plays in our mental playbook with every ounce of enthusiasm, skill, and grace we have within us. Intentionality and purpose are what will allow us to engage and activate all of these vital tools. In fact, in my dissertation study on the mental and emotional experience of the transition out of the NFL and into life thereafter, these two elements emerged as critical to life beyond football. Redefining purpose in their lives after football was gone became the ultimate challenge these men faced, but it was facilitated by an intentionality in the pursuit of that redefinition. Whether it took them twelve months or twelve years, intentionality and purpose were two of the defining forces at play.

Intentionality and purpose are essential in all the building blocks of our mental performance foundation, too. I'm hopeful this integrative concept is making more and more sense to you as we've progressed through these chapters. We must be intentional and purposeful about developing our awareness; about understanding why we do what we do, who we are, and who we are trying to become; about investing wisely in the development of our confidence; about identifying the relevant information and keeping our attention on the right things at the right time; about staying within the right optimal zone for the task at hand; about mastering our emotions; and about using mental rehearsal as a means to hone our craft. We must also, therefore, be intentional and purposeful about having effective routines that allow us to build healthy habits into our lives. For all of this to work on a macro level, intentionality and purpose must be the recurring themes on a micro level.

So, all of these concepts and skills are converging now, as we stand at this beautiful precipice of poten- tial and possibility. And we must remain intentional about our efforts to execute! Building healthy habits requires this same level of commitment.

THE CANYON

Before we dive into the actual play of **routines**, let's begin with the scientific concept of habits. Habits are things that we do so frequently that the action becomes nearly involuntary. I like to think of habits as canyons. The repeated action we've taken is like water that has carved a particular course over a long period of time and created deep canyons that makes such actions happen almost automatically. When I'm working with people on developing healthy habits, I often use this analogy, because the fact of the matter is that *all* of us have these deep-running canyons—both good and bad habits! It is the very nature of the human experience, and it is the very nature of how habits them- selves are formed over time with constant repetition. Each time we repeat an action, the "water" flows through our canyon, and the crevices become a little deeper. Continued repetition over a long period of time only makes the habits more firmly entrenched.

Let's look at an example. Say a student, desperate for a passing grade, decides to cheat on an exam. *At that very moment, the water began to flow through this new canyon.* He ends up getting a good grade on the exam, and when the next big exam comes up, he cheats again—this time with a little more ease since the process had already been set in motion. *The current of the water strengthens and the crevice becomes a little deeper.* By the following semester, the habit is forming.

This same student, also an athlete, is in the weight room one day and decides to shave off a few reps when the coach isn't looking. He does eight reps instead of ten, simply because he knows he can get away with it. Eventually, he starts cheating in other areas of his life as well; perhaps his longtime girlfriend leaves town for a few weeks, and he gets bored. His habit of cheating became more firmly entrenched every time he made the decision to cheat, which brings discord and the destruction of his principles, of his values, and of his vision of the person he wants to become. You see, the brain doesn't distinguish between different areas in our lives—in this case, whether he was in class, in the weight room, or with his girlfriend; it only knows what *habits* we've created. The canyon is wide and the water is deep.

The point is that once you develop a habit, and you repeat it consistently, you are deepening your canyon (wiring your brain) in a way that has profound and far-reaching implications that will impact how you show up for life. And it's difficult to break bad habits: the canyons within us are so deep and the water so fast-running that any change of direction requires tremendous time, effort, and attention. **But it can be done.** Yes, building new habits is hard, but it is not impossible. It just takes redirecting the water (your thoughts and actions) along a new course consistently enough that the new behavior becomes the natural response.

If we work hard to develop new routines and habits, we are eventually able to create new canyons and redirect our rhythms through **awareness**, **choice**, **intention**, and **action** to facilitate change, and you can, too . . . if you're willing to do what it takes.

Choose the life that is most useful, and habit will make it the most agreeable.

SIR FRANCIS BACON

MAKE EXCELLENCE
THE ESSENCE OF YOUR BEING

Habits lead to consistency in performance. And, ultimately, consistency leads us to excellence. When I worked at IMG Academy, I spoke to a group of about 150 young tennis players from all over the world. We were having a discussion about the importance of developing high-performance habits, and the question I posed to them was simply, "What is a habit?"

The response I received from one young man from Portugal (only fifteen years old!) still floors me to this very day. This young man stood up, and without a moment's hesitation, answered in his strong, Portuguese accent, "A habit is something that you do so often that it becomes a part of the very essence of your being." Read that again.

When I consider his perfect definition of a habit and align it with the Aristotle quote that we referenced in Brain Science 101 (**"We are what** we repeatedly do. Excellence, therefore, is not an act. It is a habit."), I am invigorated to know that *excellence, then,* can be part of the *essence of our being* if we choose to make it so.

This concept is profoundly energizing and inspiring, not just because of the possibilities and promises that lie within it, but because of its powerful reminder to *all* of us that excellence is ours for the taking. The potential to become excellent in our pursuits belongs to each and every one of us, not only elite athletes and extraordinarily high performers. Excellence is not just a word and a concept . . . it is an actionable way of existing!

What does this really *mean*, though? How do we actually *achieve* excellence? We achieve it by learning to manage our minds, our emotions, and our behaviors on a consistent basis, moment by moment. Habits are something we perform so often they become a part of who we are and how we operate. And routines are a tool that allow us to build this consistency into our performance and daily lives in a way that will drive us toward excellence.

MEDIOCRITY IS A HABIT, TOO

I once worked with a hockey player who'd recently become more aware of how his less-than-stellar habits in some aspects of his life could have direct, sustained, negative influence on other parts of his life.

"You know, Doc," he said one afternoon as we were discussing habits of excellence, "when I get ready for a game, I always dress like a pro on my way to the rink. I wear a suit, pay careful attention to my mindset and every detail of my preparation . . ." He paused thoughtfully before continuing, "But when I get in my car to go home, I've been noticing what a disaster it is. It's always dirty, inside and out. And when I get home and walk through the door, my room is the same way, like a tornado hit it. I've even noticed the people I'm hanging out with are a little sloppy; they don't know what they're trying to achieve and don't really care about their performance all that much." And then he asked the essential question: "Does all of this have an effect on my game?"

That he even asked the question made me smile, because it demonstrated he was aware of the fact that who and what he surrounded himself with, and the quality of his values, did, indeed, have an impact on how he showed up to the things that really mattered to him and did, indeed, have a *tremendous* effect on his game. This awareness, alongside our continued discussions and mental performance training, allowed him to take inventory of how his own habits spilled over into other areas of his life. Our brain does not know the difference between being at a game, in our car or room, or even with our friends; it only knows what habits we wire into our lives.

In his case, the lesson was clear: if you're sloppy and unkempt in some areas of your life and you hang out with people who display similar (or worse) habits, it will eventually bleed into the other areas of your life. My answer to him was unequivocal: "Yes, all of this *will* show up in your game!"

Yes, **mediocrity is a habit, too.** But with hard work, you can create new paths and develop new canyons through which waters will flow with positivity and grace. Refuse to let mediocrity seep into your life. Redirect its flow. Remember: **how you do anything is how you do everything.** So, every time you catch yourself putting in a mediocre performance, no matter what the task or activity, catch it and redirect it. Strive to create canyons of excellence.

Here's the bottom line: when things get difficult or when adversity strikes, we are going to automatically resort to whatever habits we have already created in our lives. **So everything you do matters.** Why?

Because you are either wiring in habits of excellence that will ensure you continue to perform highly, even when things get difficult, or you're fixing habits of mediocrity that will undoubtedly surface when your back is against the ropes.

THE VALUE OF HEALTHY ROUTINES

Routines are an effective way to help get our minds, emotions, and bodies in position to build powerful habits. In short:

Routines help build **habits** . . .

Habits lead to **consistency** . . .

Consistency leads to **excellence**.

We all have routines. We all have consistent patterns we practice and repeated rhythms we rely on throughout the course of our day. So, we must ask ourselves, "Are the routines I have in my life helping me show up as the best version of myself, consistently?" Developing effective routines is a *learned skill*; we can integrate these skills into our performance strategy and execution in way that facilitates performance excellence, but it takes work. It requires intentionality and purpose.

Positioning routines as the last building block in this sequence allows us to incorporate with more intentionality everything that we've learned to date. We turn our attention to routines here as the final play because if we can build effective routines, we can incorporate all the previous plays into this important (and acquired) skill. We can build routines around ways to ensure we are aware, to keep us motivated and confident, to help us find our optimal zone and stay focused, and to ensure that we show up calm, cool, and collected in high-pressure situations. Routines can and should be customized and retrofitted with any of the previous seven mental plays. Using these vital tools and making them a habitual part of your everyday experience will ensure that you are ready to deliver when it matters most.

Routines bring order, structure, and rhythm to our daily lives. **Heathy routines help us build healthy habits**. And building healthy routines and habits influences how we show up for life, moment by moment. Again, habits lead to consistency, and it is consistency that leads us to true excellence.

You'll remember from the previous chapter that the myelin sheath forms at the micro level and grows stronger as we repeat certain acts and behaviors. **What fires together wires together**. Habits and routines, too, can become myelinated at the neurological level. Our habits—how we think, how we show up, what we believe—are malleable and can, therefore, be managed.

THE IMPORTANCE OF FLEXIBILITY WITHIN ROUTINES

It's easy to let our routines get the best of us sometimes; they become obsessions rather than pathways to productivity and excellence. When this happens, our routines control us; we do not control them. I've experienced scenarios when athletes have had travel delays or severe weather has struck, limiting the amount of time for pre-game or at halftime preparation. In those moments, having flexible routines is critical for athletes; they need to be able to handle these sudden, unanticipated changes with poise and determination.

It's common knowledge that many athletes have pre-game routines that can become very elaborate. But when those rhythms and rituals become superstitions or create imbalance (not just for athletes but for *anyone* whose routines have become too rigid), serious issues can arise.

ROUTINES SHOULD HELP, NOT HURT

A colleague shared a story of a professional athlete who traveled overseas to compete. A *deeply* ingrained part of his routine, which became more of a superstition, was to eat his favorite candy before each game. And it had to be that *precise type* of candy. Nothing else would do.

You can probably imagine what unfolded. The athlete arrived at his overseas destination and his favorite candy wasn't available. It wasn't even possible for a team assistant to run out and buy it because the candy wasn't available anywhere in the country. His routine had become a superstition, a crutch, a distracting obsession, which severely impaired and impacted his mental game and, therefore, his performance.

The lesson is this. Our routines should exist to *help* us, not hurt us. And if what you are developing is an obsession, then you need to adapt that particular routine. High-performing environments are often fluid, changing, and dynamic. **You must train your brain to adapt quickly and develop routines and habits that will allow you to show up to these moments calm, cool, and collected, rather than compromised.** Routines must be flexible and almost *pliable*; they must fit comfortably into any situation you encounter. Never should they be a hindrance.

When coaching my clients, I always encourage them to have *at least* three types of routine: pre-game, transitions, and post-game. Now, I know we aren't all operating in a sporting context, but it's a simple framework to help us think about how we enter into a day, event, or moment; how we navigate through the experience amid the highs and lows; and how we bring the experience to its conclusion. Routines in these three areas help us create consistency and stability in all areas of our lives.

1. What's your routine to initiate an action or moment?

2. What's your routine to transition between actions or moments?

3. What's your routine to conclude an action or moment?

WHAT LEGACY DO YOU WANT TO LEAVE?

Everything you do matters. Every action you take, every routine you repeat, and every habit you cultivate impacts how you show up for life. Utilize your habits and routines so they work *for* you, not against you. Positive routines can bring order, structure, and peace to your life. Routines help get you and keep you in the right mindset so you can position yourself most strategically on your course toward excellence.

When you think about your own habits, ask yourself these questions: How deep are your canyons? And is the water that runs through them flowing in a positive direction, or are the currents carrying you away to a place you don't want to be? And when you think about your own routines, which ones do you use to get you through the day? How do they help you navigate the challenges and strains of stressful moments?

Remember that the actions we take and the mindsets we develop will endure far longer than we will. After our living moments have become memories and our physical presence is no longer, the impact of our thoughts and actions will remain. In fact, this is how we will define our legacy and how *others* will describe our legacy. We want to make sure that the legacy we leave is one of *excellence*, not *mediocrity*. Live now the way you want to be remembered. **Never leave excellence to chance.**

Creating a vision of who you want to be, what you want to accomplish, and how you want to be remembered is crucial. **Without vision, people perish.** How you want to be remembered begins with your mindset, and the habits you establish will wire your mindset (and your actions) for the manifestation of that vision; of your legacy. Every action, every drop of water that flows through your canyon, is either creating habits of excellence or habits of mediocrity. Take inventory of

 your waterways; if they are blocked or polluted, create new ones. It will take time and effort, but eventually, new ones can be formed. Your continued quest for excellence depends upon it . . . as does your legacy.

PLAY #8:
ROUTINES

CHAMPIONSHIP MINDSET TRAINING:
"Reset Your Routines"

—————

- Think about a situation at work or at home that requires you to bring your full self to the moment but is often problematic or uncomfortable. Take a few minutes to visualize yourself approaching that moment, standing in its midst, and moving through the situation until it's over.

- What routines do you usually employ before, during, and after this moment? What patterns, thoughts, or repeated behaviors do you generally follow during these times?

- Now create a few new routines that might help you navigate, diffuse, or redirect the situation. Reset your routine in a more positive direction. Begin the process of creating a new canyon. Writing it down might be helpful so that you can come back to it later to assess and evaluate.

Pre-Game Routine:

Transition Routine:

Post-Game Routine:

CHAPTER NINE

FROM THE PLAYBOOK TO THE FIELD

Let's Go!

Knowledge is of no value unless you put it into practice.

ANTON CHEKHOV

All of the plays, all of the building blocks, all of the science-based knowl-edge, and all of the awareness-based mental performance concepts we've explored throughout this book will mean little unless and until you put all of it into action in your own life. Now is your beautiful moment. Now is the time that these principles can be practiced and brought to bear. Now is the moment when one-dimensional words in a playbook transform into four-dimensional, actionable behavior on the game field of life.

Excellence is experiential. Yes, carefully studying the *principles* of excellence is an important part of the journey—after all, we've got to become aware before we can develop a full understanding of how our brain drives us toward performance excellence. But now that we have acquired this intellectual, emotional, and holistic understanding of these principles, it's time to move this entire process one vital step forward: **it's go-time**. It's time to execute. It's time to pick up our brushes and paint these vibrant colors onto the canvas of our daily lives, with wide, bold strokes that *everyone* can see and appreciate, including family, friends, colleagues, competitors, employers, or employees . . . but most importantly, *you*. You are now equipped with a playbook that includes the mental performance plays you can run, which can be integrated into the very fabric of how you live your life. The **belief** that you are educated, equipped, and empowered to win the mental game in every aspect of your life is the foundation that will allow you to be a force for good in this beautiful world. As you've learned: you must win in the mind first.

We already know that **we've got to be aware before we can enhance**—aware of our thoughts, which affect our emotions, which affect our physiological responses, which ultimately drive our performance. As we become more aware, and as we become more comfortable with the tools and principles of mental performance excellence, we suit ourselves up in the armor we need to step onto the field (any field, in any domain) with confidence, grace, and courage. And we set ourselves up to drive harder, to focus more intently, and to become more sensitive to the ways in which we must adapt to perform excellently.

All of this is a choice. And, it is a choice that begins with a single question, a single thought: "Do I want to make my life better by being bold and courageous in my pursuit of excellence?"

Developing a championship mindset is a three-step process. We stand poised, now, at the precipice of the powerful third step.

THREE STEPS TO BUILDING CHAMPIONSHIP MINDSETS

STEP 1: UNDERSTAND

We must understand the principles of championship mindsets, which begins with the solid mental performance foundation that we have explored through the eight mental plays in this playbook. If we are focusing on **mental rehearsal**, for example, the seventh play, then we must fully understand and absorb the underlying principles of perspective, vividness, control, timing and pace, and the importance of repetition.

If we're focusing on **attentional control**, the fifth play, then we must fully grasp the science of focus and completely understand and embrace the mind-body connection that must be achieved if we are to place our attention on the things that will drive our success.

So, as the first step, **understanding is vital**. We cannot properly integrate or execute until we first understand. No plan or principle can be fully, consistently, and confidently executed until it is understood.

---

*Take time to deliberate, but when the time for action
has arrived, stop thinking and go in.*

NAPOLEON BONAPARTE

STEP 2: INTEGRATE

Armed with a full understanding of these principles, we must now integrate them into our own thinking; we must weave them into the fabric of our own thoughts, our own beliefs, and our own values. Remember that it **all begins with our thoughts**, and given that we have 70,000–80,000 thoughts a day, knowing how to integrate, manage, and direct (or redirect) our thoughts is essential, not just to our ability to show up ready to perform, but to how we show up to every moment of every single day. Integration is what takes these concepts from being scientific and about others to being *yours and about you. Integration is what helps you believe you can actually be the man or woman you desire to be in this world.*

STEP 3: EXECUTE

Once we understand the principles and integrate them into our own mind and heart to truly believe we are capable, then we must execute; we must do the very things we desire to do. I'm never as interested in what people want in life (although it's important) as I am in what people are willing to *do* to get what they say that they want. Ultimately, it is about **action**; it is about **execution**.

Here is where we must execute the concepts of focus in a way that drives performance excellence by placing our **attention** on the right things, at the right time, at the right level. This is the place where we not only *identify* our optimal zone but we also *move into it!* Here is where we leverage the five keys of **confidence**. It is now when we walk onto that big stage feeling calm, cool, and collected.

The same is true for each play. When we move them into action, we blow the breath of *life* into them. We give them a pulse. It is here where we take the *desire* for excellence and turn it into *habits* of excellence.

*Well **done** is better than well said.*

BENJAMIN FRANKLIN

AN INVITATION

I have devoted my entire career to helping and teaching others to develop positive, powerful, and productive mindsets in a way that drives them toward goodness, greatness, and excellence. I've labored long and lovingly on the blueprints of this powerful, foundational program, and I am deeply blessed and gratified to know that these principles have enriched the lives of many.

But this is far more than a program; it is far more than a set of integrated principles that will change your trajectory and challenge your mind to open, expand, and soar toward previously unexplored heights. Championship Mindset Training is also value-driven, mission-focused, and deeply rooted in the unshakeable belief that **you are the architect of your own success and greatness**. You have the blueprint. Now you must run these plays and build upon the foundation.

I invite you now to use these plays, practice this training, and build your own championship mindsets with great care, attention, and *intention*. Make the move from knowledge to action. Join me on this journey to becoming the next best version of yourself that you can imagine, or that perhaps you never could have imagined . . . until now. **The world needs that version of you, right now.**

A TRAINING PLAN
FOR THE JOURNEY

In the next chapter, you will find Championship Mindset Training that brings together all the mental performance training exercises we've explored throughout the course of this book. Put them into practice. Weave them into the fabric of your every day, moment by moment.

The time for inaction, indecision, and fear is finished. It is behind you. As you begin the next chapter, you are also turning the page that will bring you face-to-face with an exciting new chapter of your life that smashes up all your old anxieties and sets you on the path to being the best you possible: the **path of action**. And it is action that will help you generate the traction you need to truly be transformed by the renewing of your mind.

Inaction breeds doubt and fear. Action breeds confidence and courage. If you want to conquer fear, do not sit home and think about it. Go out and get busy.

DALE CARNEGIE

CHAPTER TEN

CHAMPIONSHIP MINDSET TRAINING

You Have the Plays. Now Run Them.

---

*Engage and **trust** in the process.
Never leave excellence to chance.*

DR. AMBER SELKING

Now that you're fully equipped with the mental performance Xs and Os you need to launch this journey, the journey itself must begin. You must make these next moments your own. Don't just talk about it. *Be* about it.

In the last chapter, I issued the call to action. What must unfold next is the action itself. To facilitate this action, I want to present to you now a compilation of the Championship Mindset Training (CMT) exercises. These should look familiar as they are the exercises at the end of each chapter, for each of the eight plays, or building blocks. The difference is that *now* we are able to view these tools from a fully integrated perspective. You are prepared, in this moment, to embrace these exercises on an experiential level. **Excellence itself is experiential**; it is not just a word, but an *act*.

 Each of these CMT exercises correspond to each of the eight mental plays. My direct appeal to you now is to **execute the exercises with consistency and intention**. Study this playbook, run the plays, and win your mental game.

MENTAL PERFORMANCE PLAYBOOK "Xs AND Os"

PLAY #1
Awareness | *You Must Be Aware Before You Enhance*

PLAY #2
Motivation | *It Is Your Job to Motivate You!*

PLAY #3
Confidence | *Confidence Is a Choice. Choose Confidence!*

PLAY #4
Intensity Management | *Find Your Optimal Zone*

PLAY #5
Attentional Control | *You Give Power to What You Focus On*

PLAY #6
Emotional Mastery | *Control the Controllables*

PLAY #7
Mental Rehearsal | *What the Mind Conceives, the Body Achieves*

PLAY #8
Routines | *How You Do Anything Is How You Do Everything*

Figure 7: Mental Performance Playbook "Xs and Os"

PLAY #1: AWARENESS

CHAMPIONSHIP MINDSET TRAINING:
"Well, Better, Learned"

At the end of every day, get into the habit of asking yourself a short, simple list of reflective questions. Write down your answers so you can reflect on them later; writing them down will allow you to chronicle your own growth. You can even jot down the answers in this book—I want you to use this as a workbook and a practical roadmap; indeed, a playbook. Answering these questions will help set you on the path to enhanced awareness, which will set you on the path toward performance excellence. Ready? Let's go!

1. What **three things** went well today, and why did they go well?

2. What **two things** need to get better tomorrow, and how will I make them go better?

3. What is **one new thing** I've learned about myself today, and why is that important?

PLAY #2: MOTIVATION

CHAMPIONSHIP MINDSET TRAINING:
"Critical Motivation Questions"

For this exercise, reflect on the critical motivation questions and write out your answers. Return to them often as you continue on this journey; ask yourself these questions whenever you feel like you need a motivational reset, jump-start, or simple reminder of your purpose, your goals, and your legacy.

1. **Why** do you do what you do? (purpose)

2. **What** do you want to accomplish? (goals)

3. **How** do you want to be remembered? (legacy)

PLAY #3: CONFIDENCE

CHAMPIONSHIP MINDSET TRAINING:
"Power Statements"

In this exercise, develop three of your own power statements. Give it carefully thought; try to closely examine which statements best capture and convey the essence of the person you really are, or are striving to become. Keep them short and sweet. This way, they're easier to remember and also easy to jot down. Put them on a sticky note near your computer, post them on your bathroom mirror, or place them near the door as you're walking out to face the new day. Commit them to memory so that, in those moments when you need them most, all you'll have to do is draw from these new mindsets you will have wired into your brain through repetition.

You can use "I am" as a place to start your power statement, or craft something more universal, such as, "Leaders initiate contact." Let's go!!

I AM ...

I AM ...

I AM ...

PLAY #4: INTENSITY MANAGEMENT

CHAMPIONSHIP MINDSET TRAINING:
"Find Your Zone!"

- *Identify* one or two areas in your own life where you really need to deliver your best in the moment. Then, for each area, identify what your optimal zone "number" is—that is, the optimal intensity level that delivers your highest possible performance level, with one being the lowest and ten being the highest. (Remember, it doesn't matter if your number is low, medium, or high; what matters is that it allows you to deliver your best!)

- *Practice* using one or more of the strategies we've explored in this chapter to help get you and keep you in your optimal zone for that task. Practice adjusting that number as necessary, to ensure you hit your mark at the precise moment you need to.

- *Be patient.* Remind yourself that this a process, a learned behavior, and mastering it might take a little time. Be gentle with yourself as you learn. Don't become frustrated if you miss your mark; just keep trying. With repeated effort, as you already know, your skills will become stronger and the process more efficient.

PLAY #5: ATTENTIONAL CONTROL

CHAMPIONSHIP MINDSET TRAINING:
"W.I.N."

Use the coming week to begin incorporating W.I.N. into your daily regimen.

- When you're facing a task that requires optimal execution and you feel like you're being distracted from delivering your best performance, ask yourself, "What's Important Now?" (or "What do I need to focus on at this *very moment*?"). Let the answer to that question be the guide and director of your attention.

- When something goes particularly well in your life this week, you can still ask yourself another W.I.N. question: "Where must I place my focus to maintain this positive direction?" Remember that it is just as important to practice W.I.N. from a positive space! An athlete, for example, could make a huge play and stop his opponent right before the end zone. But if the athlete doesn't turn around and do it *again*, the opponent may still score a touchdown! Practicing W.I.N. keeps you executing at a high level on a consistent basis.

- Create visual reminders of your W.I.N. strategies. Write them down! Post them somewhere they can be easily seen—at your work station, on your treadmill, or even on your cleats. Train your brain to turn to W.I.N. when you need it most!

PLAY #6: EMOTIONAL MASTERY

CHAMPIONSHIP MINDSET TRAINING:
"Controlling Your Controllables"

- Identify three recurring situations in your life that are usually high pressure or stress-inducing. What do those moments *feel* like? What physiological responses do they produce in your body?

- Draw two circles. In one circle, write down the things that are in your control during each particular moment. In the other circle, write down the things that are not in your control. **Think about purposefully directing your time, energy, and attention to only the things inside your "controllable" circle.** Leave the things in your "uncontrollable" circle alone . . . but be aware that they are there.

- Again, it is important to be gentle and patient with yourself; this is a process. The more you do this, the easier it will become, but it will probably feel difficult at first.

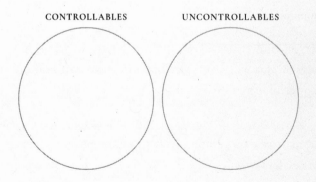

CONTROLLABLES   UNCONTROLLABLES

Figure 6: Controllables vs. Uncontrollables

PLAY #7: MENTAL REHEARSAL

CHAMPIONSHIP MINDSET TRAINING:
"5 Minutes, 5 Senses"

- Close your eyes, slow your breathing, and settle into one of your favorite memories. It can be an event from as far back as your childhood or a defining moment you might have experienced last week. Find that moment and settle in its midst. Do not rush. It sometimes takes a few minutes to find it and stand solidly at its center. Be patient with yourself during this process.

- Now that you're in it, employ each of your five senses so that you are able to bring it to life. Visualize the sights. Call up the sounds. Remember the touch. Activate your taste buds. Breathe in deeply and recall the smells. Writing them down might help enhance their clarity, at least until you become accustomed to this process. Stay in this moment for *five minutes*. This is, in fact, a long time (perhaps longer than the original moment lasted!), but it will allow you to fully focus on each sensory experience (one minute each).

- Try it for five days. Five minutes, for five days, using your five senses. This will train your brain to create vivid and, therefore, powerful mental rehearsals.

- Once you begin feeling more proficient at mental rehearsal, start using it as a preparation strategy before meetings, games, interviews, and so on.

PLAY #8: ROUTINES

CHAMPIONSHIP MINDSET TRAINING:
"Reset Your Routines"

- Think about a situation at work or at home that requires you to bring your full self to the moment but is often problematic or uncomfortable. Take a few minutes to visualize yourself approaching that moment, standing in its midst, and moving through the situation until it's over.

- What routines do you usually employ before, during, and after this moment? What patterns, thoughts, or repeated behaviors do you generally follow during these times?

- Now, create a few new routines that might help you navigate, diffuse, or redirect the situation. Reset your routine in a more positive direction. Begin the process of creating a new canyon. Writing it down might be helpful so that you can come back to it later to assess and evaluate.

Pre-Game Routine:

Transition Routine:

Post-Game Routine:

CHAPTER ELEVEN

A NEW BEGINNING

Greatness Isn't Born. It's Made.

---

*"For I know the plans I have for you," declares the
Lord, "plans to prosper you and not to harm you,
plans to give you hope and a future."*

JEREMIAH 29:11

I live life with the mindset that time is short, so we should live fast. When you are in pursuit of something incredible, why wait? Do whatever you can, whenever you can do it, with whomever will support you to pursue, with a sense of purpose and fire, that for which your heart longs. Failure along the way is inevitable when you dance on the cusp of the impossible. In fact, failure itself—if we learn from it—helps us stretch beyond the limits of impossibility. But it takes courage to live there, to dance there.

Along my journey, I integrated another mindset that was first presented to me from a colleague in my master's program. She was an incredibly accomplished woman in a variety of spaces, and she once said to me, "Amber, life is long, and you can swim deep many times." In essence, she was saying that if we apply ourselves diligently and trust the process of becoming, we never know in how many areas of life we can "swim deep" and become excellent. At first, I felt this was contrary to my notion that life was short and that I had to do all I could with every minute or it'd be over and gone and wasted. But I've learned over the course of my own high-performance journey that while different, the two perspectives are complementary: we can **be more** than we ever imagined if we go after every day with intention and purpose . . . and we can **become more** than we ever dreamed if we allow our journey to unfold into new and daring territory along the way.

WHEN NUMBERS LEAD US TO OUR DESTINY

The fact that this book has eleven chapters is not by chance. Athletes often tend to be obsessed with numbers, and I was certainly no different. My original soccer jersey number was 1 because, well, that's what I wanted to be, always and in *everything* (just ask my mama, God bless her!). When 1 was not an option in high school, I went after 11, because it was two 1s, in my mind. When I went to Notre Dame, 11 was already taken. Heartbroken, I sought consolation and guidance from my strength coach, who creatively urged me to go with 29, not only because it was his college baseball number but also because 2+9 = 11! *Genius!* Number 29 it was.

Because Notre Dame was the top-ranked team in the country, we signed things for young girls and fans nearly every day. I always signed mine, "ALatt, Jeremiah 29:11." (My maiden name is Lattner.) My thought at the time was, *Eleven was my number then, twenty-nine is my number now, and that's a good verse, should anyone actually ever read it.* Every day for nine months, that was how I signed my name. That was my identity; it was how I saw myself.

Then one spring day, right before finals began, I had my end-of-the-year meeting with my coaches. I expected to hear, "You worked your tail off this spring, and you have a lot of work to do over the summer as you come back from your knee injury, but we're excited to watch you keep growing." At least that's what the upper classmen earnestly conveyed when I sought their feedback after practices. But instead, they asked me, bluntly, "How would you feel if you weren't on the team next year? You came in with ten girls, we have another ten girls coming in this fall, and your knee just didn't really come back the way we had hoped."

I was devastated. Crushed. Everything I had done since I was seven years old was done with the end goal of playing Division-I college soccer. When I didn't readily volunteer to give up on my dream, they told me to come back in an hour and they would let me know what they had decided.

I left in tears. With no mental or emotional bandwidth to do anything else, I aimlessly checked my email. At the time, I was getting daily devotionals from the Fellowship of Christian Athletes (FCA), and they always began with a verse from the Bible. The verse that day read, *Jeremiah 29:11 "For I know the plans I have for your life says the Lord. Plans to prosper you and not to harm you; plans to give you hope and a future."*

Then I really broke down. I knew it was over. My dream was about to come to an anti-climactic, crashing halt. For nine months, I had written that verse in hopes of it inspiring someone else, but in that moment, I knew I had written it every day so that it would be etched into my heart when my whole identity stood on the brink of collapse. There was a plan . . . *trust* it. There was hope . . . *embrace* it. There would be a future . . . if I had the courage to walk toward it. This was a promise, and I *chose* to believe it.

But, little did I know that that experience of disappointment would be a critical moment in my sport psychology journey. The very thing I'd devoted an entire lifetime to achieving (playing college soccer) was suddenly gone, and I was devastated. But my passion for sport and performance psychology stems from this formative experience, and it is anchored in knowing that what is learned and applied in one's current domain can also be transferred to life after that season ends. While I know that pain and heartache come to *everyone*, especially to those who work hard to get what they want and give everything they have toward achieving their goals, I firmly believe that mental performance training helps educate, equip, and empower people to not only achieve higher levels of performance excellence with greater internal joy and fulfillment but also navigate the most adverse seasons of life with a sense of purpose, of destiny. My own identity crisis as a college athlete is also what drove my dissertation study, entitled, "When the Lights Go Out, How Do They Turn Back On?: A Classic Grounded Theory on the Transition out of the National Football League (NFL)." The study analyzed the transition experience of twelve former professional football players and then constructed a three-model theory on their mental and emotional transition experience. What I thought may destroy me became the catalyst for this whole new chapter of my life that I hope helps others in their own journeys.

Life *is* so short. It is *so* precious. The seasons of life that we all experience are fleeting, and I urge all of us to savor them. The mountaintops *and* the valleys are all set before us so that we can learn, so that we can grow, so that we can explore yet another layer of what it truly means to be a human being that has been created in the image of the Creator of the Universe. To avoid adversity, to wish it away, or to show up without the deep-seated belief and the unshakeable conviction that "this, too, shall pass" nullifies one of the greatest gifts we've all been given: **to be** *alive*.

Life is long, too. We must embrace this journey. We must trust that when one season ends, another is coming on its heels that is *intended* for us; in fact, it was planned long in advance for us. Impact and influence are not one-and-done kind of things: they are ever-evolving, developing constructs that we must allow to permeate every opportunity that stands before us. Don't settle for stagnant cycles of living. Do not conform to the patterns that this world gives us for sport, for work, for marriage, for family, or for life, but rather, be *transformed* by a constant resetting and refocusing of your mind and your heart on truth.

I pray this book has been what I intended it to be for you: **a bridge**. A bridge to your hopes and dreams; a bridge to a more grounded and holistic way of thinking about who you are today and who you are becoming for tomorrow; a bridge that carries you toward being the next best version of yourself.

Greatness isn't born. It is made. It is built. It is woven into our lives in moment-by-moment increments. As we strive, as we fail, as we adjust, as we come back after getting punched in the mouth, and as we celebrate victories, the habits of excellence that are required to succeed with grace and navigate adversity with grit become wired into the very essence of our being, little by little. And that, my friends, is true greatness: the capacity to stand in the very center of who you have been created to be, with a sense of purpose and passion, delivering consistent, high performance when it matters most at whatever you choose to put your hand toward.

THE END FOR A NEW BEGINNING

One of the most powerful experiences of my life was a pilgrimage I took through northern Spain called El Camino de Santiago, or The Way of St. James. While there were many revelatory moments along the way, I will leave you with one of the many symbols that are part of the historical legacy of this experience. On the back wall of the Cathedral of Santiago de Compostela, the two symbols Alpha and Omega are engraved. They are symbols meaning "the beginning" and "the end;" but on the exterior wall of the Cathedral, they are inverted and appear as Omega and Alpha—Ω & A—**"the end"** and **"the beginning."** As the priest said in the mass held daily for arriving pilgrims that we attended after five days of walking out on the Way, the symbols are inverted to convey the truth that **the cathedral does not mark the end of the journey, but rather the beginning.** Blessed are those who could take what they learned, what they experienced on their own pilgrimage, and apply it to their lives thereafter.

As we conclude our time together, I invite you to join me, to stay with me, to continue learning from and growing together on our journeys through this wild and beautiful world. This is not the end: it is a brand-new beginning and we must now apply what we've learned to our lives hereafter. The world needs more bridge-builders, light-bearers, and hope-dealers. The world needs you.

So, I urge you to believe in the promise of Jeremiah 29:11 and LET'S GOOO!!!

Dr. Amber Selking

selkingperformance.com

𝕏 @ChampMindsets

📷 @ChampMindsets

f SelkingPerformanceGroup

DrSelking@selkingperformance.com

---

*Some people want it to happen, some wish it would
happen, others make it happen.*

MICHAEL JORDAN

QR CODE APPENDIX

ACKNOWLEDGMENTS

One of my favorite quotes by Marianne Williamson begins, "Our deepest fear is not that we are inadequate. Our deepest fear is that we are powerful beyond measure." What we need now more than ever are courageous individuals who choose to explore the incredible power that lies within them as human beings—to learn, to grow, to influence, to contribute—to be a force for good in our beautiful world.

Aaron James Selking, my incredible husband, you are my rock. You are the steady hand and quiet supporter who gives me the courage to keep exploring my own next layer of potential. You inspire me with your genuine care for others, and you challenge me to think beyond my own frameworks. Without your constant support as I write late into the night, or while you are driving or making dinner; as I come home late because of extended talks on the football field; or as I strive to manifest the greatness I furiously feel within my spirit, I would not feel the freedom and peace to pursue what's in my heart for eternal impact. You are the one my soul loves; being your wife is the biggest blessing of my life. I love you from eternity and back, my King!

The very first person who ever saw the potential for excellence in me and then demanded it from me was my mom. Mom, I have no idea how you loved and led me along such a fine line of intensity and grace, but I am so grateful for your relentless support of my fierce identity and your unwavering commitment to helping me learn the habits necessary to be a contributing member of our world. Your example as a mom, wife, and professional are etched in my heart. I love you so much, and am so thankful for your influence. You always reminded me that my vision and goals were different than others' so that I didn't hesitate at their criticism or scorn, and that I should abound in forgiveness and grace.

Dad, you built the American Dream and proved to us kids that it can be done if you're willing to work hard enough, for long enough. Thanks for your love and support in everything I do. While I know you never really fully understood what the heck I was trying to do, I also know you never doubted that I could do it. From trusting that you'd catch me every time I jumped off of something high as a little girl to knowing you are always a phone call away today, I'll always be your baby girl.

Kyle and AshLee, you two are the best siblings a woman could ever have. You are both so gifted in your own unique ways, and you inspire me to keep learning, growing, and showing up to be the best. #BPTs.

To my late Grandpa and Grandma Lee, you both helped forge me. I love you so much, and feel so blessed to have had your influence in my life for so many years. From calling Grandma under the covers to tell her my secrets to having Papa tell me all the time while throwing the football in the back yard, "Am, if you can touch it, you can *catch* it!" I am a byproduct of your love and commitment to family.

Janice Cummings, you have always been and will always be my "Grams." I used to think that you were the bride the church refers to as the "Bride of Christ" because of the intimacy and joy you modeled through your walk with Christ. Thanks for bringing me to know Jesus as my friend and Savior, and bringing light to every person you meet.

There have been a lot of bridge-builders in my own life, and one of them is Woodie Pippens. Coach, you may have started as my strength coach, but you have become my friend, mentor, and constant fuel to my fire. Thank you for all the life lessons, for helping me explore complex topics like masculinity/femininity, spirituality, race, and the games of sport and life.

To some of my closest mentors—Red and Liz Maust, Bill Brennan, and Jimmy Connelly—thank you for your relentless support of my growth and development, from spiritual to professional to marital to personal, each of you has devoted countless hours to molding my mindset, and I feel so blessed to have such incredible people with whom to walk along this journey.

Dr. Rick McGuire—better known as simply, Coach—thank you for the hours (and hours) you've poured into my development as a professional in the field of sport psychology. While there are books to teach us science, few people are blessed with someone like you to teach them how to integrate knowledge into wisdom that can permeate the complex dynamics of human systems. You do so with simplicity and clarity, which is, in fact, how we were created to live. Fiddlers can't play without an astute teacher; I am honored to be a part of your coaching tree!

I've spent hours in the presence of Coach Lou Holtz, and every time I am amazed by his concern for others, his memory of specific moments, and his extreme generosity. Coach, thank you for allowing me share your stage for so many years, and for investing in my development during "Year 29" of my life, and beyond.

Speaking of courageous leaders, Jason Lippert, you are a true force for good who demands goodness and greatness in everything you touch. Your captivating vision and relentless pursuit of winning—first in the lives of our team members and then in business—invigorate me to keep fighting the good fight. There is no company in the world built quite like Lippert, and it's your eternally-inspired belief that we can do better that makes that possible. Thanks for believing in me, and giving me the freedom to create alongside the incredible team you have developed.

The athletes, coaches, and professionals with whom I have worked are my driving force. Your belief in your own "stirring of greatness" and the trust you so delicately extend inspire me daily to be better for you. I love you, and I love watching you grow and struggle and persevere and *become* through the process.

To all those who said I couldn't and all those who believed I could; to my faithful podcast listeners; to my clients who have become more like family.; and to my Sister Scribe, who helped intersect words with truth.

And most importantly, to my Lord and Savior Jesus Christ, the Author and Perfector of my soul. This wild journey of greatness to which You've called me has been nothing short of invigorating, and I cannot wait to see where You lead next!

May we all have the courage to walk into a reality that may indeed be powerful beyond measure.

God Bless.

Dr. Amber Selking

Dr. Amber Selking
"Jeremiah 29:11"

ABOUT
THE AUTHOR

As a leader in the field of sport and performance psychology, Dr. Amber Selking has been fiercely devoted to optimizing human performance in people and systems throughout her career.

She is the founder of Selking Performance Group, a leading performance consulting practice that helps individuals, companies, and sports teams achieve sustainable results. As her company mission proclaims, Dr. Selking is committed to "Building Championship Mindsets from the LockerRoom to the BoardRoom," working to emphasize the power of mindset and leadership in a way that synergizes people, purpose, and systems to achieve and maximize performance excellence.

She has served as the Mental Performance Coach for the Notre Dame Fighting Irish Football team, where she helped to construct a comprehensive, integrated, high-performance system and a culture of mental toughness. At the University of Notre Dame, she has also served as an adjunct professor in the Mendoza College of Business. As the Vice President of Leadership & Culture Development at Lippert, a global, publicly traded manufacturing company, she works to construct high-performance leadership systems that position business as a force for good in the world.

Dr. Selking is a sought-after speaker and lecturer, addressing organizations around the world on the topic of optimizing human performance. She hosts the popular podcast *Building Championship Mindsets*, which resonates with a global audience in many fields of expertise.

Dr. Selking holds a PhD in Educational and Counseling Psychology from the University of Missouri, a master's degree in Sport and Performance psychology from the University of Denver, and an undergraduate degree in Management Consulting with a minor in European studies and a certificate in International Business from the University of Notre Dame.

Amber grew up in the small town of Montrose, Pennsylvania, and now lives in South Bend, Indiana, with her husband, Aaron, and their Doberman Pinscher, Rockne.

Reach out today for keynote speaking, consulting, or performance coaching at DrSelking@selkingperformance.com.

Why?

~~pay bills~~

What do you want to accomplish?
learn about finance, travel

How do you want to be remembered
hard worker & good example for others especially my nieces & future nephews.